Licensed Lending in New York

LICENSED LENDING IN NEW YORK

BY

DR. JOHN M. CHAPMAN
Professor Emeritus of Banking

DR. ROBERT P. SHAY
Professor of Banking and Finance

A Report of the
GRADUATE SCHOOL OF BUSINESS
COLUMBIA UNIVERSITY

Printed in the United States of America

Contents

Tables

Charts

Preface

Our interest in undertaking this investigation of licensed lending in New York State grew out of our 1967 study.[1] While analyzing data from 30 states in 1964, we became convinced that consumer borrowers were not being served by the consumer finance industry in New York to the same extent that they were being served elsewhere. For example, that study revealed that New York ranked 23rd out of 30 states in the average amount of loans outstanding per person from lenders licensed under the small loan law.[2] In terms of the number of loans outstanding per person, New York ranked 26th.[3] Furthermore, New York had the fewest number of offices per person among the 30 states,[4] suggesting that the conditions for establishing new offices under New York's "convenience and advantage" clause were restrictive.

These facts indicated to us that the extension of small loans was being discouraged in New York. There appeared to be three possible explanations. First, it was apparent that higher risk borrowers did not obtain credit as easily as in other states because the rate structure was lower. Only 3 of the 30 states had lower ratios of bad debts to average loans outstanding than New York's ratio, suggesting that better risks were accepted in New York.[5] Second, while fewer offices per population allowed licensed lenders in New York to generate the largest average number of loans per office among the 30 states, there was less competition for borrowers resulting in fewer loans being made. Finally, the $800 limit upon the size of loan that could be made was well below the average, so that New York's licensed lenders did not generate as large an amount of credit per person as in most of the other states.

But these inferences, however suggestive, were all based upon comparisons during one year. We saw the need to investigate the trends of the small loan industry in New York for at least the past decade in order to see whether the 1964 situation was representative and whether

[1] John M. Chapman and Robert P. Shay, eds., *The Consumer Finance Industry: Its Costs and Regulation*, New York, 1967.

[2] *Ibid.*, Table 26.

[3] *Ibid.*

[4] *Ibid.*, Table 30.

[5] *Ibid.*, Table 22.

it had deteriorated or improved in subsequent years. In making the amount of loans outstanding per person our basic measure of the industry's performance in New York relative to other states, we are recognizing the following considerations: First, the past history of the small loan industry and its legislative development tell us that when conditions under which small loans can be granted become increasingly restrictive, illegal lending grows, with the consequent harassment and punitive collection tactics practiced by racketeering elements; second, legal rates of charge must be high enough to cover the costs of extending, servicing, and collecting small loans; and third, the evolution of small loan legislation has demonstrated that the best way to ensure that small loans will be made in sufficient amount to meet the needs of borrowers is to provide a rate structure which will allow competitive rates of return to be earned by stockholders of highly supervised licensed lending organizations.[6]

The latest year for which data were available for this study is 1967. The prevailing economic conditions in 1968 saw a continuation of the adverse trends affecting earnings and expenses of licensed lenders in New York. Average Loans Outstanding in New York State remained virtually the same in 1968 as in 1967, but net income, before interest, for all licensed lenders in per cent of average loans outstanding declined from 4.81 to 4.30 per cent. Interest costs increased sharply during 1968 and 1969, with the prime rate rising from 6 per cent in November 1967 to 8½ per cent in June 1969. Recognizing the strain that prevailing economic conditions were placing on licensed lenders, the New York legislature passed a bill increasing the maximum loan limit for licensed lenders from $800 to $1,400, and increasing the rate ceilings to 1½ per cent per month on balances from $300 to $900, and 1¼ per cent on balances above $900 to $1,400. On May 26, 1969, as this study was being prepared for publication, Governor Nelson A. Rockefeller signed the bill which became law on July 1.

We have not changed the text of our study to take account of this latest change in New York's small loan law. It will be apparent to the reader that the changes enacted, while granting temporary relief, are not consistent with our recommendation for fundamental changes that would increase competition in the market for higher-risk cash loans.

[6] See Rolf Nugent, "Three Experiments with Small Loan Interest Rates", *Harvard Business Review*, October 1933, pp. 35-46.

Acknowledgments

This study was made possible by a research grant from the New York State Consumer Finance Association to the Columbia Business School. In addition, the Association provided invaluable assistance by requesting its members to send us copies of data submitted to the New York State Banking Department between 1960 and 1967. Such information made it possible for us to investigate whether income and expenses varied among licensed lenders according to company size (Chapters 3 and 4).

In addition, we wish to thank members of the New York State Banking Department who supplied us with interpretations of published data, and helped answer innumerable other questions promptly and accurately. In particular, we are grateful to Vincent J. Nolan, Deputy Superintendent of Banking, for the courtesies extended to us.

Dr. S. Lees Booth, Director of Research of the National Consumer Finance Association, supplied us with data that allowed us to estimate interest income and leverage ratios for interstate companies in our New York sample based upon averages from the company-size groups published in the N.C.F.A.'s annual research report. We appreciate this assistance and advice.

We owe special acknowledgment and thanks to the Advisory Committee for their assistance in forming plans for the project, attending committee meetings, and reviewing preliminary drafts of the study. Advisory Committee member are: Alfred E. Orlin, Chairman, Guardian Loan Company, Inc.; William A. Dillon, Interlakes Finance Corporation; Harry O. Harmon, Boyd-Harmon Finance Company; William A. Hummel, American Investment Company; Lawrence Kelder, Beneficial Finance Company; Gordon J. Tomasch, American Finance Management Corporation; Richard O. Wiesner, New York State Consumer Finance Association; and Peter L. Morris, Household Finance Corporation. Other valuable assistance was rendered by Helmuth Miller, Beneficial Finance Company, and Ernst Dauer, Household Finance Corporation.

We are most indebted to our small research staff for their contribution to the study. Thomas A. Durkin, our chief research assistant, conducted the statistical investigations and tabulations. Florence Liang and James T. Fergus assisted with the tabulations and charts. Joan Donna Rabinow did the bulk of our typing with competence and irreverence. Virginia Meltzer edited the volume, and H. Irving Forman prepared the charts.

None of the persons listed above are responsible for the conclusions of this study. They, as well as any errors or omissions, are attributable to the authors.

John M. Chapman
Robert P. Shay

Conclusions

In reviewing the history of New York's small loan legislation, we found that the decision of the Banking Department to recommend a cut in rate ceilings in 1941 was crucial in limiting the loan services provided by licensed lenders to borrowers in the years which have followed. The legislature implemented the Banking Department's recommended public utility philosophy of fixing rate ceilings that would determine rates of charge at levels expected to provide a return on average employed assets of seven per cent. In subsequent years the Banking Department abandoned this standard and encountered difficulty in finding a consistent measure of a rate base. Thus, the public utility philosophy degenerated into a rather inconclusive, pragmatic evaluation of the need to provide incentive for capital to maintain a stable growth of licensed loans.

The department chose the rate of return on capital funds as its substitute for the rate of return on assets when increased reliance upon leverage by licensed lenders occurred after the end of World War II. Yet the Banking Department has never obtained realistic breakdowns of borrowed versus capital funds employed by interstate companies with operations under the small loan law in New York. Nor has it obtained realistic estimates of interest expense from these companies. Thus, while the Department has been able to evaluate the net operating income before interest and taxes to assets, it has had no direct measure of the standard it adopted to measure the financial status of the industry it regulates: the rate of return on capital funds used in licensed lending in New York.

While we urge that an improvement in reporting procedures be adopted for interstate companies, our basic concern arises from our conviction that the 1941 decision to regulate the licensed lending industry as if it were a natural monopoly was unfortunate. Pragmatically, we can point out, as we did above, that without a consistent standard for appraising the adequacy of rate ceilings, how can they be adjusted to changing economic conditions? We have noted that the 1941 rate ceilings on loans up to $300 have been frozen into a rate structure made unrealistic by the decreasing purchasing power of the dollar and the steady rise in the expenses of extending loans since 1946. The only flexible element of New York's rate ceiling structure has been the bargaining over the rate to be charged on that portion of the loan over $300 when the loan limit has been considered ready for change.

We prefer to argue, however, that the rate ceilings existing before 1941 would have better served New York's residents up to now if the Department had chosen to relax its insistence upon strict convenience and advantage standards and attacked excessive earnings rates by issuing new licenses in areas where rates of charge remained high along with earnings rates. While that was not within the spirit of the times in 1941 after the experience of the Great Depression, to continue that philosophy into the 1970's we find unthinkable, especially in view of the findings of our 1967 study of the consumer finance industry: we found that higher or lower rate ceilings as they existed in 1964 were not accompanied by higher or lower profits, but rather by changing availability of loans. The higher the rate ceiling, the more marginal the borrowers accepted, and the higher the necessity to provide for bad debts.[1] Thus, with hindsight in 1969, we aver that the 1941 decision was unfortunate and should not be carried into the 1970's.

In Chapter 2, the statistical consequences of the 1941 decision become evident, but only after World War II had ended and the subsequent peacetime decade had passed. The major statistical findings of our review of experience under New York's small loan legislation are: 1) There was no significant growth of small loans in New York until the legislature passed its version of the Uniform Small Loan Law in 1932 with a rate structure of 3-2 per cent at $150 to $300. 2) Between 1932 and 1938 licensed loans outstanding in New York grew faster than loans outstanding in the entire U.S., either from consumer finance companies or from all sources of personal loans. After 1938, licensed loans in New York grew more slowly in comparison, and the relative decline, accentuated by the 1941 cut in rate ceilings, has continued with only temporary interruptions through 1967. 3) The

[1] Robert P. Shay, "State Regulation and the Provision of Small Loans", in *The Consumer Finance Industry, Its Costs and Regulation,* John M. Chapman and Robert P. Shay, eds., New York, 1967, p. 102.

1949 and 1960 amendments to the small loan law in New York, changing both the rate and loan ceilings, occasioned the temporary interruptions to the relative decline of licensed lending in New York. 4) Other sources of personal loans in New York have grown more rapidly than loans by licensed lenders but these sources have, in the more recent years, experienced a modest decline relative to personal loans in the U.S. 5) Thus, a personal loan gap had apparently grown up in New York by 1967, occasioned by two conditions along with other unknown causes: a. restrictive rate ceilings on licensed lending and on other sources of personal loans have narrowed the market for personal loans; and b. there was virtually no institutional source for personal loans of more than $800 for borrowers who cannot qualify for loans at the 12 per cent per annum rate ceiling authorized for commercial banks and credit unions.

Given these findings, it is well known that whenever the supply of a good or service is constrained by law from meeting the demand, evasive practices or illegal markets can be expected to arise. Because of the legal barriers to the supply of loans, the practice of doubling up on loans by borrowers became more prevalent in 1968 than it had been in 1957, suggesting that the true loan limit for almost one quarter of licensed loan customers (borrowers) had moved closer to $1,600 than the legal limit of $800. Similarly, borrowing larger amounts in adjacent states (Pennsylvania and New Jersey) diverted loans away from New York lenders but allowed borrowers in New York to satisfy their demands at rates of charge above those permitted by New York's law.

We believe, however, that the legal rate ceiling and restricted entry, as well as the loan limit, are pervasive influences modifying the growth of licensed loans, and probably personal loans as well, in New York. We hope that both the Banking Department and the legislature in New York will recognize that New York's legal rate ceiling results in the denial of loans to many credit-worthy citizens who have the ability to repay but who, as members of a class of borrowers, require higher costs of investigation and collection than borrowers currently acceptable under existing law. This is the unfortunate aspect of the misapplication of the public utility philosophy of regulation to licensed lending in New York, as indicated by our fragmentary data comparing loan approval and population per licensed loan office ratios in offices located in disadvantaged areas with those in other areas.

Our analysis of the financial status of licensed lenders in New York between 1960 and 1967 in Chapters 3 and 4 indicates that the licensed lending industry can be kept alive with alternating periods of prosperity and stagnation following adjustments in the small loan law. We were able to demonstrate that the need for relief at the end of 1967 was probably greater than the need for relief in 1960. Our findings relative to the 1960-67 experience indicated that: 1) The combination of rising operating expenses and declining gross income as related to average outstandings reduced the rate of net income before interest and taxes. This squeeze in net income was accentuated by rising costs of borrowed funds, especially in 1966 and 1967.[2] 2) No commensurate rise in the volume of business occurred after 1961 to offset the declining margin of profit, although increased trading upon equity may have partially cushioned the effect on the estimated return to capital. Yet our estimates of the return to capital indicate a decline to levels below those estimated for 1960.

It would appear that the time has come to consider fundamental changes in small loan legislation in New York instead of adopting changes that result in a few years of financial health followed by the customary period of financial decline. We consider reevaluation of the entire rate ceiling structure to be essential, with special attention given to raising rate ceilings on loans of $300 and under.

Even more important is a basic shift in philosophy that would permit competition to become effective in the market for higher-risk cash loans. We believe the rate ceiling structure proposed in the Uniform Consumer Credit Code (UCCC)[3] to be workable in New

[2] The rising cost of borrowed funds has been even more pronounced since 1967, as interest rates reached historically high levels in 1969.

[3] As promulgated at the annual meeting of the National Conference of Commissioners on Uniform State Laws, July 22 - August 1, 1968, Englewood Cliffs, 1968. The rate ceiling structure proposed for closed-end loans (and closed-end sales credit) limit finance charges to:

a. The total of
   1. 36 per cent per year on that part of the unpaid balance of the amount financed that is $300 or less;
   2. 21 per cent per year on that part of the unpaid balance of the amount financed that is more than $300 but does not exceed $1,000; and
   3. 15 per cent per year on the unpaid balance of the amount financed that is more than $1,000; or

b. 18 per cent per year on the unpaid balance of the amount financed.

See sections 3.508 and 2.201.

York, but only if the related considerations involving free entry are enacted and basic adherence to the basic principles underlying that model law is maintained. The UCCC is a model law approved by the National Conference of Commissioners on Uniform State Laws on July 30, 1968, and by the American Bar Association on August 7, 1968.[4] It will receive consideration by the various state legislatures in ensuing legislative sessions.[5]

[4] The revised final draft of the UCCC appears in the CCH Installment Credit Guide No. 191, extra ed., December 12, 1968.

[5] For recent appraisals of the UCCC, see the entire issue of "Consumer Credit Reform," *Law and Contemporary Problems,* Vol. XXXIII, No. 4, Autumn 1968; and Robert P. Shay, "The Uniform Consumer Credit Code: An Economist's View," *Cornell Law Review,* Vol. 54, No. 4, April 1969.

I

An Introduction to Licensed Lending in New York

A Brief History of Small Loan Legislation in the U.S. and in New York

Following the Civil War, increased urbanization occurred with the growth in industrial development in New York as in other states. The concomitant growth of the wage earning class also signaled the increased interdependence among individuals whose subsistence was no longer supplied directly by products grown on one's own farm. Emergencies, occasioned by illness or unemployment, often depleted the meager, limited amounts of savings held by members of the laboring class. During the period when the usury laws prevented legitimate lenders from offering small loans at rates consistent with their cost, wage earners could turn only to relatives and friends before they were driven to the illegal lenders, who came to be known as loan sharks.

During the three decades before 1916, efforts were made to develop meaningful legislation that would meet the growing demands for small loans. These efforts began with attempts to ensure that loans were made within the usury laws' rate limits by cracking down on violations. Such attempts were called the "prohibitive theory" and did not succeed in eliminating loan shark activity.[1] Subsequent legislative attempts

[1] See David J. Gallert, Walter S. Hilborn, and Geoffrey May, *Small Loan Legislation,* Russell Sage Foundation, New York, 1932, pp. 27-28. See pp. 55ff for the contribution of the Russell Sage Foundation to the formation of remedial loan associations.

were devoted to stimulating semiphilanthropic agencies to enter the small loan business. When too few of these agencies came into being to combat the flourishing activities of loan sharks, the Russell Sage Foundation, which had long been actively interested in combating loan sharks, finally developed the regulated and supervised commercial theory under which a specially licensed and supervised group of lenders were allowed to establish rates of charge that would cover costs and attract capital to be invested in small loans.[2] In 1916, the Uniform Small Loan Law (USLL) was drafted as a model act by the Russell Sage Foundation with the assistance of the American Association of Small Loan Brokers. Thirty-two years of trial and error experimentation in small loan legislation led the framers of the USLL to accept the following principles, which still underlie most such legislation today:

1. The (small loan) business was recognized as a public necessity.
2. To obtain sufficient capital to supply this necessity the law had to allow the business to be conducted on a commercial basis, and to authorize a return which would attract into the field enough capital to supply the needs of borrowers.
3. This return had to be above the usual legal contract rate and the conventional banking rate of the state.
4. In consideration of this higher return on loans, the business had to submit to public supervision and regulation.
5. Such supervision and regulation were necessary to prevent the lenders from abusing their privileges and to protect the section of the public most needing protection.
6. The law had to contain certain regulations for the conduct of the business, which experience had shown to be necessary.
7. The law had to govern all loans below a certain amount, except such as were otherwise specially regulated by law.
8. The penalties of the law had to be such that the law would be effective.[3]

[2] *Ibid.*, p. 89.

[3] *Ibid.*, p. 88.

The first state small loan law, passed in Massachusetts in 1911 before the USLL was drafted, anticipated many of its provisions. The first three states to enact the model bill were Indiana, Illinois, and Maine, in 1917. The USLL was revised periodically by the Russell Sage Foundation in the light of experience. Such drafts were issued in 1918, 1919, 1923, 1932, 1935, and 1942. Russell Sage discontinued its activities in the small loan field after World War II. Subsequent model acts have been developed periodically by the National Consumer Finance Association. Today, laws in 47 of the 50 states bear similarity to the draft of the USLL that was recommended at the time each of the statutes was enacted.

New York State enacted a law in 1895 allowing corporations that limited their dividends to make loans up to $200 to persons at a rate of 3 per cent per month for the first two months and thereafter at 2 per cent per month, plus a fee of $3.00.[4] In any year no such corporation could declare more than a 10 per cent dividend on its capital stock but, after the corporation had accumulated a surplus equal to 50 per cent of its capital, the superintendent of the banking department was empowered to reduce the rates of charge to whatever levels would produce a 10 per cent return on its capital stock.[5]

The New York State Banking Department later evaluated this first attempt to combat the loan sharks in 1895 as a failure and, indeed, added that minor amendments over the next forty years did not improve matters.[6] But during the period 1929-32, the State Banking Department, the Baumes Crime Commission, the Russell Sage Foundation, the Attorney General, and representatives of other interested agencies urged the state legislature to enact effective small loan legislation. This general reaction in favor of new legislation was due in part, no doubt, to the shocking disclosures that usurious interest rates, ranging from 240 to 520 per cent, had been charged, resulting in payments of more than $25,000,000 in interest by New York wage earners in 1928.[7] In 1929, 1930, and 1931, bills were introduced to revise the New York

[4] *Ibid.*, p. 24.

[5] *Ibid.*, p. 25.

[6] *Special Report of the Superintendent of Banks on Licensed Lenders*, State of New York Banking Department, 1946, p. 7.

[7] *Credit for the Consumer*, New York State Finance Association, 1956, p. 13.

Small Loan Law but, despite the support of the groups named above, they failed to pass.[8]

In 1932 the bill was again introduced in the New York legislature. Governor Franklin D. Roosevelt sent a special message to the legislature "certifying to the necessity for immediate passage."[9] The bill was passed by the unanimous vote of both the Senate and Assembly and signed by the Governor on March 26, 1932. The law became effective on June 1.

Thus, it was not until 1932 that the New York legislature embraced the fundamental principles of the USLL, enacting legislation permitting licensed lenders to make loans up to the amount of $300 with a rate of 3 per cent per month on the first $150 of the loan balance and 2½ per cent per month on that part of the loan balance above $150 (hereafter designated as 3-2½ per cent at $150 to $300).

With respect to this legislation, the Banking Department later commented:

> In 1932 the Legislature decided to place the making of these loans on a commercial, rather than a philanthropic basis. This change recognized that the best way of meeting the loan shark evil was to allow an adequate return to carefully regulated companies. As a result, little has been heard of the loan shark in recent years. Profit margins of lenders have been reduced by rate cuts, but the attractiveness of the small loan field for the employment of capital remains.[10]

There have been four changes in the rate and loan size limits in New York's small loan law since 1932. In 1941, the rate structure was lowered to 2½-2 per cent at $100 to $300. In 1949, the maximum size of a loan was increased to $500 and the rate structure became 2½-2 per cent at $100 and ½ per cent at $300 to $500. In 1960, the maximum loan size was increased to $800 and the rate structure was made 2½-2 per cent at $100 and ¾ per cent at $300 to $800.

[8] *Ibid.*, p. 15.

[9] *Ibid.*, p. 16.

[10] *Special Report of the Superintendent of Banks on Licensed Lenders*, 1946, p. 8.

Rationale for Rate and Loan Size Changes in New York's Small Loan Law

THE 1941 CHANGE IN RATE CEILINGS

Before each of the changes in the Small Loan Law since 1932, the New York State Banking Department has issued a report analyzing the performance of licensed lenders since the previous change in the small loan law. The Department's first such report in 1940 recommended that maximum rates be cut to the extent "that a rate of return of about 7 per cent on assets employed in the small loan business is fair and reasonable and adequate to encourage the continued employment in this field of capital already invested.[11] On this basis the Department concluded "that a maximum rate of 2½ per cent per month on loan balances not exceeding $100.00, and 2 per cent per month on balances in excess of such amount will permit licensed lenders to operate in this State at a fair rate of return on invested capital."[12]

Experience between 1932 and 1938 indicated that the rate structure enacted in 1932 had, indeed, been successful in attracting capital to the extension of small loans. Loans outstanding at the close of the year grew from $10,102,000 in 1932 to $55,501,000 at the end of 1938.[13] The number of licensees grew from 78 to 269 over the same period.[14] Although there were continued proposals for drastic reductions in rates of charge in the state legislature, the Banking Department postponed its consideration of possible revision until the 1940 report when it noted that "licensees have been in operation long enough (between 1932 and 1938) to make their reports useful for reconsideration of the rate question."[15]

In reaching their decision to recommend a lowering of rate ceilings, the Banking Department had to choose between two regulatory philosophies. They could allow rate ceilings to remain relatively high, at

[11] *Special Report of the Superintendent of Banks of the State of New York Relative to Licensed Lenders*, 1940, p. 17.

[12] *Ibid.*, p. 21.

[13] *Ibid.*, p. 7.

[14] *Ibid.*, p. 7.

[15] *Ibid.*, p. 7.

the 1932 levels, and depend upon competition for new offices to establish lower rates, or set rate ceilings at levels low enough to assure themselves that with fewer offices most borrowers would be charged rates at the ceiling level. The 1932-38 experience had demonstrated that a substantial proportion of borrowers received below-ceiling rates, but the department was not willing to live with the rate patterns that existed in 1938 (illustrated in Table 1). They commented as follows:

> However, rate competition appears to have been spotty. In a few areas, notably in the central business districts of large cities, competition has been quite effective in reducing rates of charge and in limiting profits and there is some evidence that licensees who continued to charge the maximum rate in those areas had to take less desirable credit risks. But in many other areas, notably in towns in which there are only one or two licensees and in locations outside the central business districts of larger cities, licensees used their semi-monopolistic position to maintain maximum charges and high earnings. There were 33 places, exclusive of commuting towns, which had but one licensee, and 27 of the licensees so situated were charging the maximum rate.[16]

The department recognized two crucial relationships in the small loan business in their analysis. First, the level of earnings was directly related to the height of the rate of charge which, in turn, reflected the extent of competition. Second, they also recognized that lenders with the higher charges under competition would be forced to accept a higher average level of risk among their customers. Yet there was a competitive solution to their dilemma which they disregarded. It was to increase the number of licensees in those areas where the higher profits were being earned and where, certainly, there would be a greater demand for licenses. In rejecting this solution, the department stated:

> While recognizing competition to be an important factor affecting rates, the Department believes that an excessive number of licensees in a given area may tend to increase operating costs and to restrain rather than encourage rate competition. In the communities which have but one licensee it is doubtful that the granting of additional licenses for the purpose of

[16] *Ibid.*, p. 16.

TABLE 1
Extent of Rate Competition by Size of Place, 1940

Places	Number of Licensees in Rate Class[a]				Net Earning Ratios[b]	
	1	2	3	4	Average[c]	Range
New York City	48	6	26	19	10.07	-2.1 to 16.9
Commuting area	9	1	8	4	11.98	4.3 to 14.8
Buffalo, Rochester, and Syracuse	2	4	7	9	11.62	5.2 to 13.6
Places of 50,000 to 149,999 population	3	3	8	5	11.46	7.5 to 15.5
Places of 30,000 to 49,999 population	10	n.a.	n.a.	n.a.	15.07	11.7 to 16.3
Places of less than 30,000 population	20	3	4	1	13.76	5.7 to 19.5
Group Totals, Average and Range	92	17	53	38	11.25	-2.1 to 19.5

[a] Rate class 1 includes those charging the maximum rate — 3 per cent a month on the first $150 and 2½ per cent a month thereafter; rate class 2 includes those charging 3 per cent to $150 and 2 per cent thereafter or approximately equivalent rates; rate class 3 includes those charging 3 per cent to $100 and 2 per cent thereafter; and rate class 4 includes those charging still lower maximum rates.

[b] Net earning ratios are net earnings, before interest but after taxes, in per cent of average employed assets.

Source: *Special Report of the Superintendent of Banks of the State of New York Relative to Licensed Lenders*, 1940, p. 16.

n.a. = not available.

[c] In per cent.

creating competition would produce the desired results. Instead such a policy would be likely to increase the overhead of the business and destroy the margin of earnings which creates the possibility for competitive reductions in charges. In view of this fact, it seems desirable to effect a reduction in the maximum rates permitted to be charged, rather than to attempt to achieve the objective of lower rates through the licensing of additional lenders to operate in fields which in the main appear already to be adequately served. If such action tends to restrict the flow of increased capital into this field, the results, in the opinion of the Department, will be largely beneficial since the services of licensed lenders are already available to most communities.[17]

[17] *Ibid.*, p. 17.

Yet the department did not recognize that their recommendation to cut rates would decrease the average level of risk that could be accepted by lenders in attempting to meet the demands of borrowers. Implicitly, by stating that some restriction on the flow of capital would be largely beneficial, the department may have thought that the average level of risk being accepted was too high, but this inference is quite remote from the language of the report. But whether or not the department desired such an effect, the ratio of net bad debt charges to average loans outstanding declined appreciably from the 1936-40 levels, both in the immediate war years and in the years that followed.[18] The real cost of the decision to cut rates in 1941 was to make loans less available to borrowers who could previously qualify for credit between 1932 and 1940.

The regulatory philosophy chosen by the Banking Department was similar to that adopted in the regulation of public utilities in that it used rate ceilings to set rates which would allow a publicly prescribed annual return of 7 per cent on a rate base. The rate base cited in the 1940 report was average employed assets, calculated by the Banking Department from estimates of total employed assets obtained by multiplying the estimated average loan balances by 115 to approximate "used and useful assets" in the small loan industry.[19] This regulatory approach allowed a continuation of the policy of restricting the number of loan offices, especially in smaller communities where it was felt that allowing additional licensees to operate would raise the costs per dollar of loan balances outstanding as demand conditions would not allow offices to be used at capacity levels.

The department's choice of a ratio of net earnings to average employed assets of 7 per cent as the basis for computing the rate ceiling structure represented a reduction of more than one-third of the average

[18] *1946 Report on Licensed Lenders, op. cit.*, Table 11, p. 43. Between 1936 and 1944, the ratios were:

Year	*Per Cent*	*Year*	*Per Cent*	*Year*	*Per Cent*
1936	2.79	1939	2.48	1942	1.76
1937	2.42	1940	2.28	1943	1.98
1938	2.77	1941	1.99	1944	0.56

Between 1957 and 1967, the ratios ranged between 1.26 and 1.69.

[19] *1940 Special Report, op. cit.*, pp. 8-11.

ratio of 11.25 per cent earned by licensees in 1938. If a "normal period" had followed adoption of the rate structure, some judgment might have been made by the department as to the adequacy of the formula used to calculate the rate ceiling structure. But World War II intervened, and the sharply decreased volume of lending that ensued prevented any real analysis of the effects of the change until well after the war had ended. This was unfortunate because, as subsequent materials analyzed in this study will show, the public utility philosophy of rate regulation applied to the consumer finance industry has resulted in a continuing decline in the incentive to bring capital into the consumer finance industry in New York State. The department justified the continued decline in incentive by shifting the basis they used to calculate the return needed to attract capital. The basis chosen in each instance permitted the department to freeze the 1940 rate ceiling changes into the rate ceiling structure, which, as we shall see, has continued to the present.

THE 1949 CHANGE IN THE SMALL LOAN LAW

The Banking Department's *Special Report on Licensed Lenders,* published in 1946, was undertaken for two reasons.[20] First, the department felt that the operating experience of licensees should be reviewed to see if any adjustment in the rate structure was needed. Second, the department wished to reexamine the basis for the $300 loan size limit as part of a broader review of the law to see whether the licensed lender business required any legislative adjustment other than in rates.

In its 1946 report, the department did not return to its 1940 stipulation that a 7 per cent ratio of net earnings to average employed assets would be needed to "encourage the continued employment in this field of capital already invested."[21] Instead it shifted its focus to three measures of the attractiveness to capital in licensed lending: (1) the ratio of earnings to used and useful assets[22] (calculated as 115 per cent of average outstanding loans), (2) earnings to equity capital, and (3) earnings to total capital. The department noted that there had been an unfavorable record of experience between 1941 and 1944 on

[20] *Op. cit.*, p. 7.

[21] *Ibid.*, p. 7.

[22] See note 10.

all three measures,[23] but, despite this record stated "that it does not believe the licensed lenders need a higher profit than they are now receiving to make the small loan field in New York State an attractive outlet for capital."[24] It is not possible to compare the 1940 estimate of the return on average employed assets of 11.25 per cent with the 1941 estimated 9.70 per cent return on assets used and useful since the methods of adjusting the data reported as expenses by reporting companies differed and the 1946 study was based upon a sample of "representative companies" that accounted for 87.8 per cent of the licensed lender business in 1944.[25]

To support its conclusion, the Banking Department turned to a comparison of returns on total capital, after taxes, of the "more than 2,600 leading corporations included in the earnings computation of the National City Bank of New York," the U.S. Treasury figures for all active corporations, the Federal Deposit Insurance Corporation data for all insured banks, and the Banking Department's calculations for licensed lenders operating in New York (see Table 2).

It is difficult to rationalize the department's position concerning relative profitability on the basis of the data in Table 2. The department noted that the figures for profitability of corporations during the war period were unusually high while licensed lenders' returns were adversely affected by the war.[26] Hence, the department expected some reversal of the record in the postwar period, especially with the expected improvement in licensed lender volume when wartime restrictions, including consumer credit controls, were lifted. But, it is

[23] Earnings in each instance are after taxes but before interest on borrowings. See the Appendix, "Note on Asset Bases," to the *1946 Report on Licensed Lenders. op. cit.*, p. 25ff.

	Return on		
Year	*Used and Useful Assets (per cent)*	*Total Capital After Taxes (per cent)*	*Equity Capital After Taxes (per cent)*
1941	9.70	9.20	11.74
1942	9.35	8.77	11.14
1943	7.47	5.66	6.74
1944	7.47	5.65	6.76
4 yr. Average	8.50	7.17	8.86

[24] *Ibid.*, p. 21.

[25] *Ibid.*, Table A, p. 14.

[26] *Ibid.*, p. 18.

TABLE 2
Net Return on Total Capital

Year	Leading Corporations	All Active Corporations	Insured Banks	Licensed Lenders
1935	5.1	7.4	n.a.	n.a.
1936	7.4	4.7	n.a.	n.a.
1937	7.2	4.9	5.8	n.a.
1938	3.8	2.3	4.4	n.a.
1939	6.2	4.3	5.6	n.a.
1940	7.4	5.0	5.7	n.a.
1941	9.2	6.9	6.8	9.2
1942	8.7	7.8	6.5	8.8
1943	8.6	7.5	8.8	5.7
1944	8.2	7.0	9.7	5.7

Source: *1946 Special Report of the Superintendent of Banks on Licensed Lenders*, p. 18.

n.a. = not available.

important to note that the significance of the 1940 reductions in rate ceilings were not judged in the light of the criteria developed in the 1940 report, while the department's estimates of the future were, necessarily, highly tentative. To this point, the department noted:

> The rate of return realized by licensed lenders and its significance with respect to rates are being constantly analyzed by the Banking Department. If it appears that the small loan rates in this State are producing profits for licensed lenders beyond those which are earned by the general run of corporations able to compete successfully for capital in the investment market, the Department will recommend an adjustment in rates to the Legislature. Conversely, if the rates should prove to be fixed too low for the preservation of adequate small loan facilities, the Department will believe itself under equal obligation to call that fact promptly to the attention of the Legislature. For it is greatly in the public interest that conditions not be made favorable for the return of the loan shark.[27]

The department recommended an increase in the loan ceiling from $300 to $500 to meet the loan requirements of the person of modest income, particularly the wage earner, because income payments, factory payrolls, average weekly earnings of factory workers, and whole-

[27] *Ibid.*, p. 18.

sale prices had all risen substantially since 1940.[28] The department was unwilling to go beyond the $500 limit because of the existence of other institutions authorized to make larger loans under its jurisdiction. Those mentioned were industrial banks, credit unions, and the personal loan departments of commercial banks. The department's philosophy of segregating the market for personal loans is well illustrated by the following quotation:

> These other instrumentalities are authorized to make the larger loans at rates of interest substantially lower than licensed lenders charge. There is no need for creating duplication and overlapping of loan facilities by permitting licensed lenders to cater to income groups able to obtain credit elsewhere at rates that are but one-half to one-quarter of those charged by licensed lenders.[29]

It is apparent that the department again did not take into consideration that the rate ceilings imposed upon these other institutions would preclude them from serving the higher risk customers who dealt with consumer finance companies. Nor did the department state that it did not believe that such demand, if it existed, should not be supplied. It had not learned, at least as far as the public record is concerned, that borrowers would "double up" on loans from licensed lenders by getting the maximum amount permitted from one licensee and then getting the remainder of his needs from a second licensee. Such procedure was not illegal and therefore the loan size limit was easily evaded by anyone willing and able to pay the price. Licensed lenders obtain information from their lenders' exchanges about multiple borrowing from small loan companies, allowing them to assess the borrower's ability to repay the combined amounts before approving the loan.

In order to establish a rate structure consistent with the $500 loan size limit, the Banking Department recommended a downward revision of existing rate ceilings, which the State Legislature did not accept when it changed the law in 1949. The department recommended that "the best adjustment of rates from the standpoint of public policy would be to reduce the present charge of 2½ per cent per month on amounts up to $100 to 2 per cent, thereby making the 2 per cent rate applicable to all amounts of $300 or less. On the unpaid balances above $300 permitted by the increase in the loan limit to $500 the

[28] *Ibid.*, p. 19.
[29] *Ibid.*, p. 20.

rate should be 1 per cent."[30] The department made its calculations on the basis of its earnings and expense data for the 1941-44 period and estimating that "with loans up to $500 a gross interest charge of approximately 23.5 per cent a year would have provided the lenders with an average net return of about 6 per cent on total capital. . . ."[31] The legislature allowed the previous rate structure of 2½ per cent per month on loans up to $100 and 2 per cent per month on loans above $100 to $300 to remain as it was, and added a rate of ½ per cent per month on loans above $300 to $500.

At this point it is apparent that the department either wanted to discourage the making of small loan sizes by proposing a reduction in rate ceilings on loans up to $100 or else it believed that licensed lenders would continue to make such loans on the basis that they could average out the higher returns from larger loans within the ceiling limit. The latter explanation ignores the fact that businessmen, even those operating under regulatory pressures, must make their loans where they can earn profits, and those loans which they know cannot be made on a profitable basis will only be made reluctantly, if at all. Using the department's 1940 calculations the 2 per cent rate of charge could only yield a 7 per cent net earnings ratio on average employed assets when the loan size was between $230 and $300.[32] In calculating the rate structure recommended in 1940 and enacted in 1941, the department recognized that with a 2½ per cent rate, loans of less than about $90 cost too much to produce the desired yield but it expected that the margin of profit on larger loan balances would compensate for the inadequacy of the rate permitted to be charged on very small loans."[33]

The statistical record in the three years that followed supported the department's contention that licensed lenders would continue to meet the demand for loans in the loan size range where rates were not sufficient to provide the target rate of return. Where 40 per cent of the number of total loans were made in the $100 or less group in 1940, the proportion remained relatively high – 34 per cent in 1941,

[30] *Ibid.*, p. 21.

[31] *Ibid.*, p. 21.

[32] *1940 Special Report of the Superintendent of Banks of the State of New York Relative to Licensed Lenders*, Chart 13, p. 38.

[33] *Ibid.*, p. 19.

38 per cent in 1943 and 1943, and 34 per cent in 1944.[34] In later years when postwar price increases decreased the purchasing power of a $100 loan, the proportions of the number of loans made dropped to 16 per cent in 1949 and to 6 per cent in 1957.[35] Thus, the short-run response to the 1940 rate cut was not appreciable possibly because the rate cut affected all loan sizes and the margins of profitability on loans of all sizes were affected. But as the twin cutting edges of inflation made themselves felt – shifting the demand from smaller to larger loans as purchasing power declined, and inflating costs of extending credit at the same time – both the incentive to demand and supply loans in smaller amounts decreased. It is fortunate that the State Legislature did not enact the department's recommended 2 per cent rate ceiling on loans up to $100 in 1949 as the availability of such loans could have virtually disappeared.

With respect to rates of charge, the department reported the following results from the 1941 rate ceiling decrease:

> At the end of 1944, though, the maximum rates were in effect in all of the 270 licensed lender offices except nine. These nine offices had only 2.10 per cent of the average loans outstanding. In no case was a rate below 1¾ per cent a month charged. The four office charging 1¾ per cent a month included two operated by a philanthropic organization. Five companies charged two per cent a month on all balances.[36]

It is apparent that rate competition came to an end in New York State when the department cut rate ceilings and restricted the number of new offices to achieve the desired return on the rate base selected.

In its 1946 report the Banking Department disregarded the unfavorable trend in previous measures of the net return to assets or capital to reach its conclusion that the return to capital remained attractive. Alternatively, the department relied primarily on a comparison of rates of return on total capital earned by licensed lenders in New York with similar rates earned by insured banks and corporations. Finally, the department adopted the philosophy that the demand for loans of all sizes would be met if the average incentive to capital were maintained, provided that above-average rates of return were made available on larger loan sizes to offset the below-average rates of return on smaller loans.

[34] *1946 Special Report of the Superintendent of Banks on Licensed Lenders,* Table 5, p. 38.

[35] *An Analysis of the Licensed Lender Industry, New York State, 1945-57,* New York State Banking Department, 1957, Table 7, p. 19.

[36] *1946 Special Report on Licensed Lenders,* p. 11.

Underlying the department's position in the 1946 report was its continued determination to restrict the number of offices so that each could operate at lower costs consistent with the lower rate levels. In short, the department was willing to support a semimonopolistic position in lending provided that profits could be limited and the lower-cost operations closely supervised. It promised to allow a rate structure that would allow returns to capital competitive with those in other regulated and unregulated industries.

THE 1960 CHANGE IN THE SMALL LOAN LAW

More than ten years elapsed before the New York Banking Department initiated another special study of possible changes in the Small Loan Law. The stimulus to the Banking Department's report, covering operating experience between 1945 and 1957, came from a bill introduced in the Legislature on February 19, 1957, sponsored by the New York State Consumer Finance Association.[37] The bill was passed by both Houses but was vetoed by the Governor on the grounds that the Banking Department had not had sufficient time or opportunity to study the industry's proposals which were based on a research study by John M. Chapman and Frederick W. Jones.[38]

The Banking Department's analysis of the intervening period between 1945 and 1957 differed from its preceding reports. It concentrated upon evaluating the industry's proposals for changes in the law rather than recommending changes of its own. The licensed lender industry's legislative proposals were summarized by the Banking Department report as follows:

> 1. Ceiling and Rate Adjustment: The 1957 bill proposed that the maximum size loan allowed by statute be increased from the present $500 to $1,000; and that the maximum rate of charge on loan balances be changed. Existing law provides that licensed lenders may charge no more than 2½ per cent per month on unpaid balances up to $100, 2 per cent on the next $200 of such balances, and ½ of 1 per cent on any remaining balance up to $500. The industry would leave the rate charge on balances up to $300 unchanged, but recommends that it be permitted to charge

[37] *An Analysis of the Licensed Lender Industry, New York State, 1945-57,* New York State Banking Department, 1957, p. 1.

[38] *An Analysis of the Current Financial Status of Licensed Lenders in the State of New York,* New York State Consumer Finance Association (mimeo), 1957, and revised October 1958.

1 per cent on balances over $300 and up to the new suggested loan ceiling of $1,000.

2. Precomputation of Interest: The bill further proposed that existing law be changed to permit interest to be precomputed at the statutory monthly rate on scheduled unpaid principal balances and added to the principal of the loan, with each payment applied to the sum of principal and precomputed interest. Included are provisions for refunding unearned charges in the event of prepayment, and default charges in the event of delinquency.

3. Credit Life and Property Insurance: The bill provided that group credit life insurance be sold to the borrower under limited and identifiable charges. Under this, the licensee could sell insurance on the life of a borrower at a proposed charge of 50 cents per $100 per year of the face amount of the obligation unless a different amount is authorized by regulations of the Superintendent of Insurance, subject to refund on prepayment. Other provisions permit the lender to sell insurance on certain types of collateral securing the loan, as well as permitting automobile liability insurance to be provided on an optional basis.[39]

The Banking Department's analysis conceded many of the points raised by the industry in their discussion of the bases for loan ceiling and rate adjustments but qualified any implicit endorsement of these proposals in ways that would caution the legislature against their uncritical acceptance. It seems relevant here to point up the logical development of the department's position in the light of their preceding reports.

Rate Ceiling Changes. With respect to need to attract capital, the department noted the steady decline after 1948 through 1956 in three measures of earnings: net income after taxes but before interest as a per cent of (1) average loans outstanding, (2) average balance sheet assets, and (3) total capital.[40] While noting its past (1940) statement of the need for a net profit of 7 per cent on assets, the department observed that the ratio had declined to 4.82 and 4.98 in 1956 and 1957, respectively.[41] However, the department again shifted toward the return on equity, after taxes but before interest, as a better

[39] *An Analysis of the Licensed Lender Industry, op. cit.*, p. 2. In addition there were miscellaneous provisions covering investigation and license fees that were administrative in nature.

[40] *Ibid.*, Table 12, p. 31.

[41] *Ibid.*, pp. 42 and 31.

measure. Here, too, however, the return had dropped substantially from 9.20 in 1941[42] to 4.81 and 4.97 per cent in 1956 and 1957.[43] Yet the Chapman and Jones study of 1957 had pointed out that comparing net earnings with reported capital funds did not provide a true measure of capital since companies that operated in more than one state could allocate whatever proportion of interest, borrowings, and capital it wished in its report to the state.[44] Reestimates of the return by Chapman and Jones based upon the capital structures of the five largest national companies were cited by the Banking Department as "acceptable data" and showed the decline seen in the table below:

Net Income as a Per Cent of Equity Capital,
Licensed Lenders in New York State,
1950-57

Year	*Per Cent*
1950	17
1951	15
1952	14
1953-57	13

Source: *An Analysis of Licensed Lenders, op. cit.*, p. 42.

Again, the Banking Department disregarded the downward trend and focused, as it had in the 1946 report, on comparative rates of return with financial and nonfinancial corporations drawn from the First National City Bank estimates. It concluded that, on this basis, the "licensees' New York State operations compare favorably with nationwide operations of all other major industries in the United States."[45]

Other conclusions reached by the Banking Department concerning the performance of licensed lenders during the 1945-57 period were:

> 2. The fact that earnings and dividends per share for a major portion of the small loan industry have been increasing and that surplus accounts have been strengthened, suggests that this industry can compete favorably with others in the capital markets.
>
> 3. The energy with which chains have been absorbing offices of other companies suggests that they are desirous of expanding rather than withdrawing capital from the field of operations in this State. While according

[42] *1946 Special Report of the Superintendent of Banks on Licensed Lenders, op. cit.*, Table A, p. 14.

[43] *An Analysis of the Licensed Lender Industry, op. cit.*, p. 31.

[44] Chapman and Jones, *op. cit.*, p. 13.

[45] *An Analysis of Licensed Lenders, op. cit.*, p. 43.

to industry spokesmen, this has been attributed to anticipation of a liberalized licensed lender law, the absorptions have also occurred during periods when there was little if any prospect of any legislative changes.

4. National chains at the close of 1957 comprised 73 per cent of the offices, owned 82 percent of the assets, and accounted for nearly 84 per cent of total net income (before taxes and interest) of the licensed lender industry in New York State. Yet, New York State operations accounted for only minor portions of their total nationwide business. Therefore, aggregate earnings of the largest licensed lenders will not be vitally affected by any legislative action in New York State. At issue, therefore, is whether industry capital will continue to be attracted to New York State in volume commensurate with public need—or whether loanable funds will seek the more generous returns available in states which have liberalized both the ceiling and rate structure. The past history of the industry taken as a whole reveals that the latter alternative is not without precedent in other states.[46]

These arguments, taken together, provide an interesting application of the department's regulatory theory of rate ceilings for licensed lenders. The theory was to limit entrance into the industry so that rate ceilings could be set low enough to ensure that borrowers were able to get loans at rates consistent with minimum costs – such costs would provide returns for the most efficient lenders that would continue to attract their capital to the state. But such rates would only allow loans to be granted to borrowers whose risk was consistent with the relatively low permissible rates of charge.

The Banking Department was content for the growth of outstanding loans to be slower than in the rest of the nation as long as the incentive to supply capital remained adequate to meet their criterion for public need. But the department failed to develop a consistent, reasonable standard for measuring capital incentive. The initial measure based on a return to average employed assets was inadequate when the industry increased the proportion of borrowed funds in their capital structure. By shifting to return on equity, the Banking Department could not develop a reliable statistical measure of equity capital from their reported data in order to base their rate structure analysis upon it. Finally, they shifted their attention to the performance of those national lenders that appeared to be most willing to invest

[46] *Ibid.*, p. 5. More recent evidence suggests that four of the largest consumer finance companies invest a larger proportion of their funds in states where their profit opportunities are larger. See Chapman and Shay, *op. cit.*, Table 29 and pp. 116ff.

their funds in New York under the restrictive conditions. But these conditions were restrictive only as long as the department ignored the need for legislative changes in the small loan law. Each of the changes made in 1949 and 1960 provided a temporary easing of the declining attractiveness of investing funds in New York. And the large chains could find more protection from competition in New York than in other states where regulation was more permissive.

Our concern is both with the declining relative position of the New York small loan industry in the nation and with the fact that the rate structure does not allow licensed lenders to serve a larger portion of the population that cannot qualify for loans in New York. Our state has a large underprivileged segment of its population that will, hopefully, emerge from a condition of poverty in the same way that upward economic mobility has always allowed our immigrant population to avail themselves of the use of small loans when they developed the capability to repay. We fear that in New York, the underprivileged have greater incentive to patronize illegal lenders in poverty areas and, if these are not readily available, to patronize the low-quality retail stores that will offer credit at legal rates but inflate the prices of their goods to cover the real costs of credit plus whatever exploitation can be added.[47] This has been the real cost of the 1940 decision of the Banking Department to emphasize a low rate ceiling structure and by-pass competition as a means of keeping profits down. The solution of setting ceiling rates low enough to keep the return on capital competitive for those allowed to compete in a semimonopolistic environment does not provide small loan services to higher risks where the need is greatest. Nor did the bill presented to the 1957 legislature by the New York State Consumer Finance Association recognize this defect in the New York Small Loan Law. As we have seen, it sought rate relief only in the upper portion of the loan sizes requested – loans between $300 and $1,000.

Loan Ceiling Changes. The Banking Department did not contest strongly the industry's proposals for an increase in the loan ceiling but did not recommend any specific limit in its report. After listing nine reasons supporting a loan ceiling increase, it contented itself with only one moderating qualification:

[47] See *The Poor Pay More,* David Caplovitz, New York, 1963, pp. 16-20.

> i. Whatever the realities which may imply a ceiling increase, it is believed that a number of states in setting very high ceilings apparently have either unknowingly violated or ignored the precepts inherent in the meaning of the *small loan* industry. Not to be overlooked in any deliberations are the original purposes of small loan legislation which would militate against overly liberalized ceilings.[48]

Of interest in the arguments favoring some increase in loan ceiling was the department's recognition that evidence of multiple borrowing indicated further pressure against present legal loan maxima. The department presented data indicating "that approximately 18 per cent of all open accounts at small loan licensees (offices of 2 large, national personal finance companies) were doubled with other lenders."[49] It was also reported that over 60 per cent of the doubled loans were made when the original loan was made at the ceiling maximum of $500.[50]

The Banking Department also expressed a belief that loan ceilings applicable to licensed lenders should be maintained at lower levels than those affecting other lenders. It noted that the maximum loan size for personal loan departments of commercial banks had been increased from a sliding scale ranging from $500 up to $2,500 based upon population to a flat ceiling of $5,000 irrespective of population.[51] But the department did not espouse absolute equality in loan ceilings. They stated:

> While discrimination is not involved here, this difference in treatment originated with a concept of separate domains for licensed lenders as against other consumer lenders. This sharp distinction has, however, tended to diminish. The licensed lender clientele today, comprises more than escapees from the loan shark. There is less to differentiate the licensed lenders' customers from those of commercial banks today than in the past.
>
> At the same time, to raise the licensed lender ceiling poses the question of possible competition with personal loan departments of banks. Some commercial banks may feel competitive inroads but lower rates and higher ceilings will continue to attract the type of borrower they have serviced in the past.

[48] *An Analysis of Licensed Lenders, op. cit.*, p. 3.

[49] *Ibid.*, p. 20.

[50] *Ibid.*, p. 20.

[51] *Ibid.*, p. 20.

> While it may not be desirable to eliminate or weaken institutional distinctions, there is merit in the view that licensed lenders be given an opportunity to share in a portion of the expansion potential which has been enjoyed by other lenders. As was shown in Chart A, growth in the licensed lender industry over the postwar period has lagged behind that of competing institutions in the field of consumer finance.[52]

It is surprising that the department did not recognize that one reason that licensed lender clientele were less differentiated from bank customers was the restrictive nature of the rate structure, especially in the smaller loan sizes. The incentives to make the larger loans close to ceiling limits could have been changed if a higher rate were permitted for loans of $300 or less. Again, the 1940 decision to cut the rates that existed between 1932 and 1940 encouraged closer competition between banks and licensed lenders. But we do not view closer competition between banks and licensed lenders as undesirable. The differences in the rates that have existed have probably been sufficient to separate the two markets according to the credit worthiness of borrowers. But there is greater recognition today than there was in 1940 that competition is not an evil to be avoided or minimized among financial institutions. Indeed, banking regulations have been liberalized both with respect to entry into banking markets and with respect to the kinds of business that banks are allowed to enter. We concur in the application of a liberalized competitive standard to licensed lenders, particularly in the current instance when market segmentation has resulted in the provision of restrictive services to small loan borrowers in New York.

Precomputation of Interest. With respect to the industry's request for precomputation, the Banking Department was disposed to acknowledge the benefits that would be brought to the licensed lenders but to stress the disadvantages to the borrowing public. They concluded:

> In reviewing the results of utilizing precomputation, certain advantages to lenders are recognized. These include: additional revenue due to the method of refunding unearned interest charges; reduced operating expenses because of increased employee efficiency; improved public relations; and the placing of licensed lenders on a par with other consumer lending institutions which use precomputation.

[52] *Ibid.*, pp. 20 and 22.

> However, an analysis of precomputation indicates substanial disadvantages to the borrowing public, the most important being that the cost to the borrower is substantially greater under precomputation than under the present method if the loan is refinanced before maturity. This is significant since approximately 80 per cent of all loans are refinanced. Additional costs to the borrower arise from default and deferred charges levied in the event of late payment, which are designed to compensate the lender for not having use of the amount of the instalment due for the period of delinquency.[53]

Precomputation was permitted in the 1960 change in the small loan law for those lending offices that wished to utilize it. In addition to raising gross income because of refinancing accounts and lowering costs of servicing accounts, precomputation had an important accounting effect in that it accelerated the speed at which interest income was collected from the borrower and taken into earnings. This advance in the timing of the earned portion of interest income by itself did not increase revenues but caused operating income to rise substantially although temporarily, as we shall see, shortly after the 1960 legislation went into effect.[54]

Credit Life and Property Insurance. The Banking Department approved in principle the industry's request to sell credit life and property insurance to borrowers in amounts up to the amount of the total unpaid indebtedness (for life insurance) and the reasonable value of the loan collateral. The department found the proposed credit life insurance charge of 50 cents per $100 per year of the face amount of the obligation excessive in its calculations of the profits that could be expected to accrue. But the stipulation that when a different amount was authorized by the Superintendent of Insurance, it would prevail, was clearly more acceptable to the Banking Department since recently promulgated maximum monthly premiums established by the New York State Insurance Department were graduated according to cost

[53] *Ibid.*, p. 5.

[54] When the same amount of interest income is earned faster, gross income is increased in the earlier portion of the period of indebtedness and lowered in the later period when precomputation is allowed and income is earned according to the rule of 78. For an explanation of this rule and comparison with alternative rules, see M. R. Neifeld, *Neifeld's Guide to Instalment Computations,* Mack Publishing Company, Easton, Pennsylvania, 1953, p. 183.

considerations from 44 to 64 cents per $100 according to the average amount of insurance in force on all debtors of a creditor.[55]

With respect to the pricing of insurance the Banking Department stated:

> b. Both the industry and the Banking Department are agreed in principle that there should be no profit on the sale of insurance to borrowers . . .
>
> c. Analysis of earning and costs based on annual charges to the borrower, ranging from the 50¢ cited in the bill down to 40¢ per $100 of initial indebtedness, indicates that profits would accrue to the licensed lenders throughout, although under certain assumptions, a 40¢ rate could entail some losses. At a 44¢ rate, which under this bill would be about the maximum that a borrower could be charged, based upon existing New York State Insurance Department regulations for group policies of $5 million or more, some net profits would still accrue to lenders.
>
> d. In evaluating these results, it should be recognized that there has as yet been no experience in this state as to the effects of permitting licensed lenders to insure their borrowers. Therefore, prudence dictates the desirability of a rate that will still leave a *small* degree of slack to absorb possible unfavorable mortality experience. In view of this, should licensed lenders be given the power to offer credit life insurance to their borrowers, it might be desirable to provide that, after perhaps three to five years, this entire question of charges to the borrower be re-examined in the light of the actual experience in New York State.[56]

The 1960 change in the small loan law permitted licensed lenders to sell credit life insurance in an amount up to the total unpaid indebtedness on the date of death and the licensee may collect a premium computed on the total amount of the indebtedness, chargeable in accordance with the rate filings made with the Superintendent of Insurance. The licensee may require a borrower, on loans of $250 or more, to insure tangible personal property, except household goods serving as collateral, for an amount not to exceed the reasonable value of such property. The premiums for all such insurance cannot exceed the premiums chargeable in accordance with rate filings made with the Superintendent of Insurance.[57]

[55] *An Analysis of Licensed Lenders, op. cit.,* p. 81.

[56] *Ibid.,* p. 6.

[57] For a more precise statement of the law as enacted, see Article IX of the Banking Law of the State of New York with Respect to Licensed Lenders, Section 357-a.

The insurance provisions of the law, as adopted, were substantially the same as requested in the 1957 bill, with the deletion of the proposed charge of 50 cents per $100 per year of the face amount of the obligation.

The Enactment of the 1960 Changes in the Small Loan Law. The New York State Legislature resolved the remaining differences between the lending industry and the Banking Department by authorizing that the loan ceiling be extended from $500 to $800, and that the rate on that portion of the loan between $300 and $800 be increased from ½ to ¾ per cent. Both the loan ceiling and the rate ceiling increases represented a compromise with the $1,000 loan ceiling and the 1 per cent rate ceiling requested on loans in the largest loan size portion of the graduated rate structure. With the additional features of the right to precompute interest income and the ability to sell credit life insurance, the 1960 changes in the small loan law were to provide temporary relief for licensed lenders who had to operate under increasingly restrictive conditions after 1941.

Conclusion

With the completion of this review of regulation in the licensed lending industry of New York, one can better understand why the extension of small loans has been discouraged in the state. First, the regulatory philosophy of the New York State Banking Department stressed the stabilization of the industry after a period of growth and development between 1932 and 1940. Second, the application of this regulatory philosophy curtailed lending to higher risks, as indicated by declining net bad debt charges as a per cent of average loans outstanding. Third, the choice to continue limiting entry to preserve semimonopolistic conditions in order to make low rate ceilings effective limited the competition for borrowers.

Under these restrictions, it is not surprising that New York ranked low in 1964 among 30 states in the number and amount of loans outstanding per person, that it had the fewest offices per unit of population, and that its bad debt ratio was among the four lowest in the nation. The restrictive rate structure, limited entry, plus the relatively low loan size limit has harnessed the licensed lending industry and its customers over the years since 1940.

Subsequent changes in the small loan law in 1949 and 1960 have provided only temporary relief, primarily by increasing the maximum loan size but also, in the 1960 change, by raising the rate ceiling in the maximum loan size bracket. But the rate ceiling structure continued to penalize the borrowers and lenders desirous of making small loans in favor of encouraging the making of larger loans by keeping the 2½ per cent rate ceiling on loans up to $100. The Report of the Joint Legislative Committee to Investigate Rates on Small Loans recognized the importance of this point in their recommendation to the New York State Legislature in January 1941. They stated:

> On the basis of the figures presented by the Superintendent of Banks there can be little doubt that the maximum rates recommended by him would discourage the making of very small loans. However commendable his desire to reduce rates of charge for all classes of borrowers, the worthy intent of such legislation, if enacted, would offer little comfort to those who might thereby be deprived of the right to borrow from lawful lending agencies. The Committee is convinced that it is in the public interest to use a revision of the maximum rate as the means of compelling licensed lenders to specialize still further in the denomination of loans which are neglected by other types of lending agencies. For this reason it recommends retention of the present maximum rate of 3 per cent per month on the first hundred dollars of any loan and reduction of the rate on any remainder to 2 per cent per month.[58]

We shall turn now to statistical verification of our hypothesis about the financial status of licensed lending in New York. For the most part we shall devote our attention to experience between 1960 and 1967, although we shall consider the statistics of earlier periods whenever they are relevant.

[58] *Report of Joint Legislative Committee to Investigate Rates of Interest on Small Loans*, New York State Legislature, Albany, 1941, p. 29.

II

Trends In Personal Loans in New York and in the U.S.

Licensed Lending in New York

Analysis of the statistical record in New York supports our interpretation of the history of regulation. First, we shall note that no significant growth of small loans in New York occurred until passage of the 1932 legislation. Second, between 1932 and 1938, licensed loans in New York grew faster than loans outstanding from consumer finance companies in the U.S., followed by a relative decline in their growth thereafter. The relative decline was accentuated after 1941 when the reduction in rate ceilings by New York State occurred. Third, the 1949 and 1960 amendments to the small loan law provided only temporary interruptions to New York's declining trend of licensed loans outstanding.

New York's delay in accepting the Uniform Small Loan Law's regulated and supervised commercial theory of licensed lending provides an apparent explanation of the decline from 19 per cent in 1914 to 1 per cent in 1930 in New York's share of loans outstanding from regulated small loan companies (Chart 1 and Table 3). The large rise from 1 to 3 per cent in 1931 probably represented the anticipated passage of a revised small loan law based on the Russell Sage Foundation's model law.[1] The 1914 to 1930 decline in New York's share of

[1] This interpretation was suggested in the *1940 Special Report of the Superintendent of Banks of the State of New York Relative to Licensed Lenders*, p. 7.

CHART 1
Regulated Small Loans Outstanding Held by Licensed Lenders in N.Y. Compared to Regulated and Total Personal Loans in U.S., 1914-40

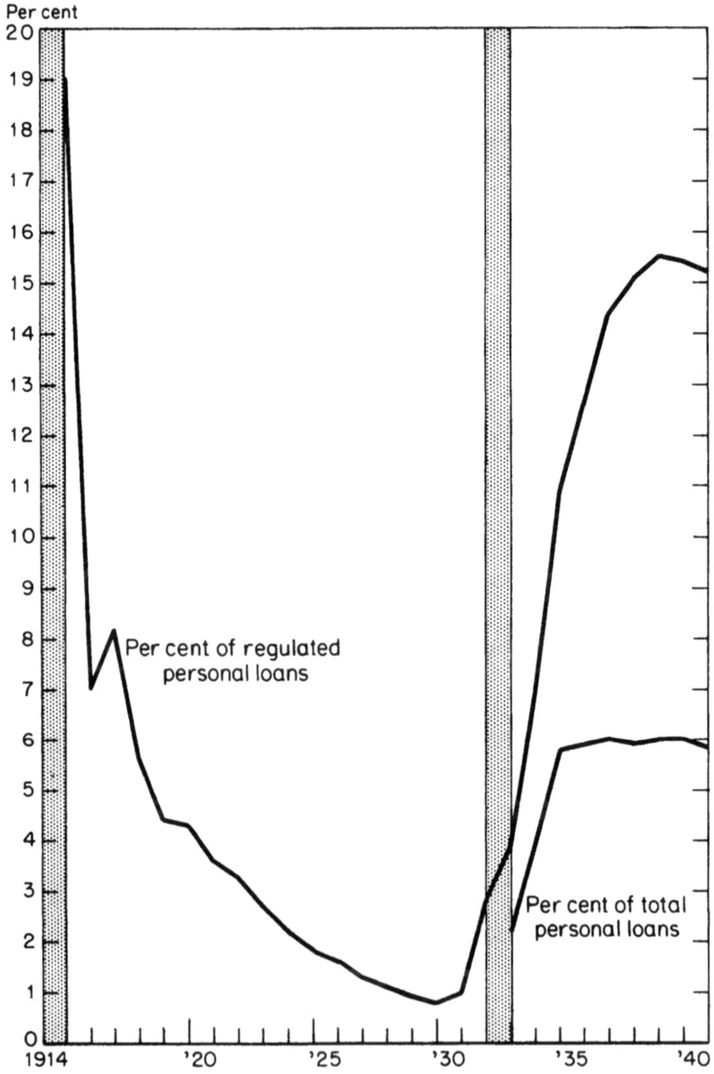

Source: Table 3.

Note: Shading denotes years in which amendments were made in the New York law.

TABLE 3

Regulated Small Loans Outstanding Held by Licensed Lenders in N.Y. Compared to Regulated and Total Personal Loans in U.S., 1914-40

(thousands of dollars)

Year	Year-End Loans Outstanding at Regulated Small Loan Companies in N.Y. (1)	Year-End Loans Outstanding at Regulated Small Loan Companies in U.S. (2)	Year-End Outstanding Personal Loans U.S. (3)	Col. 1 ÷ Col. 2 (per cent) (4)	Col. 1 ÷ Col. 3 (per cent) (5)
1914	528	2,762	n.a.	19.1	n.a.
1915	645	9,249	n.a.	7.0	n.a.
1916	761	9,260	n.a.	8.2	n.a.
1917	881	15,771	n.a.	5.6	n.a.
1918	791	17,748	n.a.	4.4	n.a.
1919	876	20,142	n.a.	4.3	n.a.
1920	887	24,345	n.a.	3.6	n.a.
1921	985	30,000	n.a.	3.3	n.a.
1922	950	35,716	n.a.	2.7	n.a.
1923	985	44,709	n.a.	2.2	n.a.
1924	1,024	55,936	n.a.	1.8	n.a.
1925	1,173	74,821	n.a.	1.6	n.a.
1926	1,307	98,277	n.a.	1.3	n.a.
1927	1,544	137,191	n.a.	1.1	n.a.
1928	1,803	193,101	n.a.	.9	n.a.
1929	1,986	263,205	n.a.	.8	n.a.
1930	2,993	287,121	n.a.	1.0	n.a.
1931	8,233	288,816	n.a.	2.8	n.a.
1932[a]	10,102	256,555	464,000	3.9	2.2
1933	16,108	232,004	416,000	6.9	3.9
1934	26,723	245,464	459,000	10.9	5.8
1935	34,007	267,085	572,000	12.7	5.9
1936	43,498	301,001	721,000	14.4	6.0
1937	53,067	351,071	900,000	15.1	5.9
1938	55,501	357,100	927,000	15.5	6.0
1939	65,134	421,900	1,088,000	15.4	6.0
1940	72,269	475,800	1,245,000	15.2	5.8

Source: 1914-37, cols. 1 and 2, R. Nugent, *Consumer Credit and Economic Stability*, Table 58, pp. 388-389; 1929-67, col. 3, Board of Governors of the Federal Reserve System; 1938-67, col. 1, N.Y. State Banking Department; 1938-48, col. 2, M. R. Neifeld, *Trends in Consumer Finance*, Easton, Pa., 1954, p. 19; 1949-67, Board of Governors of the Federal Reserve System.

[a]First N.Y. law modeled on USLL.

n.a.—not applicable.

the market represented a rise in dollars from $.5 million to $3 million in New York contrasted with a greater national increase from $2.7 million to $287 million in the nation. These were the years when other states were adopting statutes based upon the Uniform Small Loan Law, allowing rates of 3 or 3½ per cent per month on the unpaid balance. New York's law, still attempting to attract capital on a semiphilanthropic basis under lower rate ceilings, could only generate a limited volume of lending.

As suggested earlier, the 1932-38 growth of licensed lending in New York, observed in Chart 1, led to a marked expansion, from 4 to 15½ per cent, in New York's share of the regulated small loan companies' personal loans. The 3-2½ per cent at $150 to $300 rate ceiling allowed the licensed lenders to approve credit risks similar to those accepted in other parts of the nation.[2] It is interesting to note that a

[2] Those who question the relation between rate ceilings and the assumption of risk should consider Rolf Nugent's analysis:

> In practice the necessity for these decisions by lenders tends to develop a set of rules of thumb whereby applicants for loans are classified with some degree of uniformity into an acceptable class and an unacceptable class depending on the amount of interest permitted. Since the state, by determining the maximum interest rate, is the arbiter of the approximate point where this division shall occur, applicants to whom lenders are unwilling to lend at the maximum rate but to whom they would be willing to lend at a higher rate are effectively denied the right to borrow by the state even though the decision is made by the lender.

Nugent calculated the effects of rate reductions in three states that lowered rate ceilings from 3 to 1½, 3½ to 2, and 3½ to 2½ per cent, respectively, between 1929 and 1931:

Estimated Ratio of Loans Made and Refused, Under the Reduced Rates, to Loans Which Would Have Been Made Under the Former Maxima in New Jersey, West Virginia and Missouri

	Per Cent by Outstanding Volume		Per Cent by Number of Loans	
	Made	Refused	Made	Refused
New Jersey	17	83	10	90
West Virginia	24	76	18	82
Missouri	86	14	70	30

Source: "Three Experiments with Small-Loan Interest Rates," *Harvard Business Review*, October 1933, pp. 38 and 40.

For an empirical test demonstrating a positive relation between credit losses and rate ceilings in 1964, see Maurice B. Goudzwaard, "Price Ceilings and Credit Rationing," *Journal of Finance*, March 1968.

CHART 2
Regulated Small Loans Outstanding Held by Licensed Lenders in N.Y. Compared to Regulated and Total Personal Loans in U.S., 1940-67

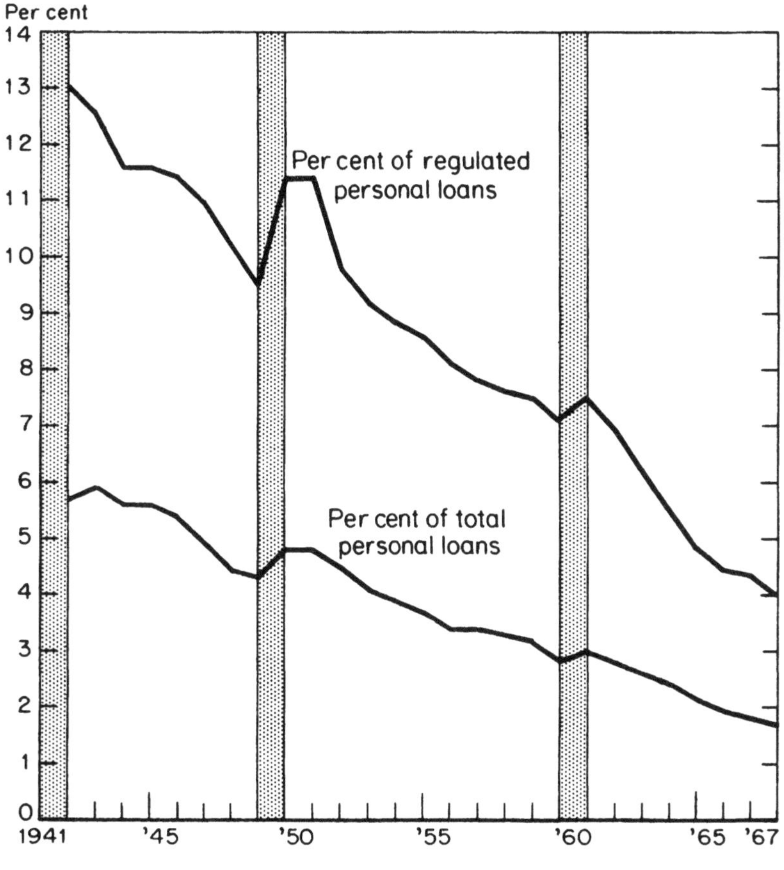

SOURCE: Table 4.

NOTE: Shading denotes years in which amendments were made in the New York law.

second declining trend in New York's market share of consumer finance company personal loans and total personal loans in the U.S. began in the latter part of the 1930's. At this time, the relative growth

TABLE 4

Regulated Small Loans Outstanding Held by Licensed Lenders in N.Y. Compared to Regulated Small Loans and Total Personal Loans in U.S., 1941-67 (thousands of dollars)

Year	Year-End Loans Outstanding at Regulated Small Loan Companies in N. Y. (1)	Year-End Loans Outstanding at Regulated Small Loan Companies in U. S. (2)	Year-End Outstanding Personal Loans U. S. (3)	Col. 1 ÷ by Col. 2 (per cent) (4)	Col. 1 ÷ by Col. 3 (per cent) (5)
1941[a]	75,510	582,000	1,322,000	13.0	5.7
1942	57,834	458,700	974,000	12.6	5.9
1943	46,592	402,100	832,000	11.6	5.6
1944	48,807	421,800	869,000	11.6	5.6
1945	54,806[b]	479,500	1,009,000	11.4	5.4
1946	73,747	670,800	1,496,000	11.0	4.9
1947	84,487	831,200	1,910,000	10.2	4.4
1948	94,941	997,400	2,224,000	9.5	4.3
1949[c]	118,036	1,038,000	2,431,000	11.4	4.8
1950	135,728	1,195,000	2,814,000	11.4	4.8
1951	151,357	1,541,000	3,357,000	9.8	4.5
1952	168,988	1,845,000	4,111,000	9.2	4.1
1953	185,521	2,118,000	4,781,000	8.8	3.9
1954	198,107	2,296,000	5,392,000	8.6	3.7
1955	210,517	2,594,000	6,112,000	8.1	3.4
1956	231,313	2,977,000	6.789,000	7.8	3.4
1957	253,991	3,335,000	7,582,000	7.6	3.3
1958	259,835	3,455,000	8,116,000	7.5	3.2
1959	268,377	3,799,000	9,386,000	7.1	2.8
1960[d]	322,534	4,300,000	10,617,000	7.5	3.0
1961	331,369	4,799,000	11,673,000	6.9	2.8
1962	353,809	5,668,000	13,414,000	6.2	2.6
1963	367,946	6,748,000	15,618,000	5.5	2.4
1964	378,433	7,837,000	17,848,000	4.8	2.1
1965	395,778	8,962,000	20,412,000	4.4	1.9
1966	410,401	9,524,000	22,187,000	4.3	1.8
1967	404,897	10,211,000	24,018,000	4.0	1.7

Source: See source for Table 3.

[a]1941 rate ceiling decrease.

[b]Estimated.

[c]Maximum loan ceiling increased from $300 to $500.

[d]Rate ceiling and loan size increase ($500 to $800).

of year-end outstanding loans in New York leveled off and began to drop behind that of the cash lending business elsewhere. The 1941 change in the law accentuated New York's relative decline until, by 1967, New York's share of the consumer finance companies' personal loans had dropped back to 4.0 per cent, about where it was in 1932 (Chart 2 and Table 4).

The amendments to the small loan law in 1949 and 1960 only interrupted the declining trend briefly. It took only three years after 1949 and one year after 1960 for New York's market share to drop below the share in the year preceding the amendments to the law. We believe that the fundamental cause of divergence in the growth rates of regulated lending in New York and the nation comes from the relatively low rate ceiling and restricted entry as well as from the limitation in loan size in New York. The low rate ceiling curtails loans to poor credit risks because the provision for loss and related extra expense of servicing loans must be curtailed when rates are lower. In short, the low rate ceiling structure must be offset by lower costs in order to provide the incentive for capital to be employed in granting loans to a wide spectrum of borrowers, classified according to risk. In New York, the spectrum served by licensed lenders must be narrower than in the nation because of the relatively low rate ceilings.

Rate and Loan Ceilings Under Effective Small Loan Laws in 47 States

New York's rate ceiling on January 1, 1968, was well below the median rate ceiling for 47 states with effective small loan laws tailored on the Uniform Small Loan Law.[3] New York's rate ceilings ranged from 83 per cent of the U.S. (47 states) median for a $100 loan, to 75 per cent for an $800 loan (Chart 3 and Table 5). The slope of New York's rate ceiling structure is similar to the naton's median rate ceiling structure, with differences ranging between 5 and 7 percentage points below the U.S. median. Such large differentials place New York's rate ceiling close to the lowest in the nation. It is the lowest for loans of $500, $700, and $800. It is next to the lowest for a $600 loan and second from the lowest for a $400 loan. Finally, it is fourth from the lowest

[3] Arkansas, Delaware, and Tennessee are the three exceptions.

CHART 3
Comparison of Median Yields of Selected Loan Sizes Under State Small Loan Law Rate Ceilings with New York's Licensed Lender Rate Ceiling, Early 1968

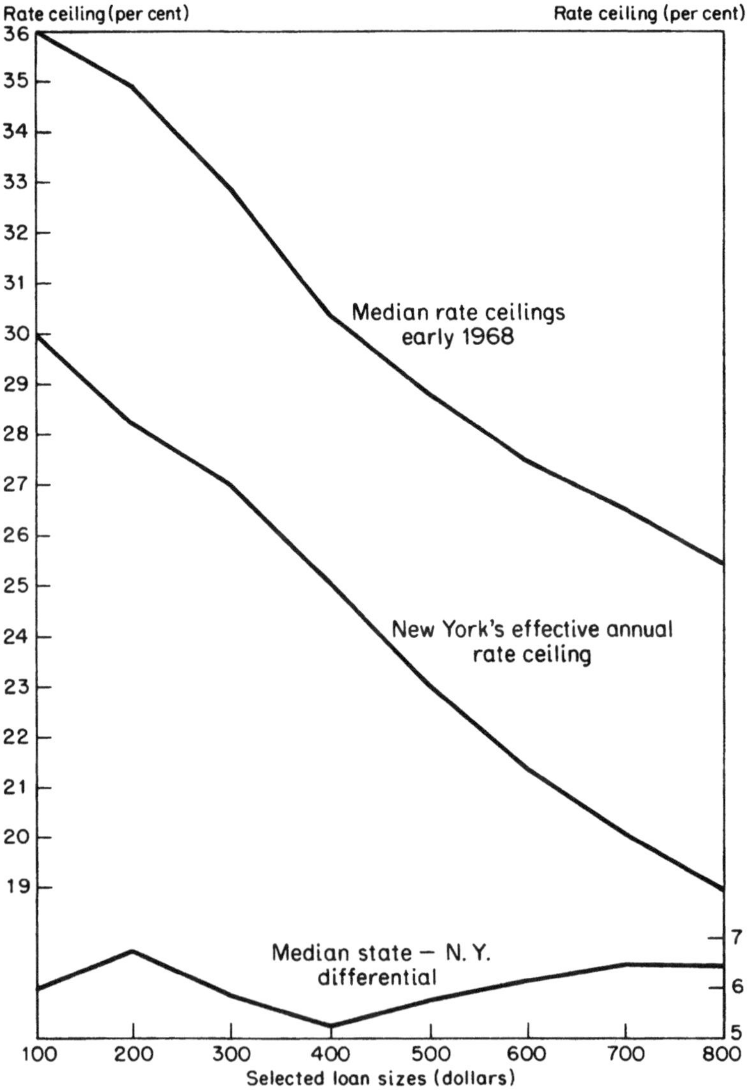

SOURCE: Table 5.

TABLE 5

Comparison of Median Yields of Selected Loan Sizes Under State Small Loan Law Rate Ceilings With New York's Licensed Lender Rate Ceiling, Early 1968

Cash Advanced to Borrowers (dollars)	Number of State Small Loan Laws	Median Rate Ceilings Early 1968 Cost[a] (per cent)	New York's Effective Annual Rate Ceiling (per cent)	Median State Rate Ceiling Less New York (per cent)	New York's Rank by Level of Yield[b]
100	47	36.00	30.00	6.00	35-43
200	47	34.92	28.20	6.72	43-44
300	47	32.88	27.00	5.88	43
400	41	30.36	25.08	5.28	39
500	41	28.80	23.08	5.76	41
600	41	27.48	21.36	6.12	40
700	35	26.52	20.04	6.48	35
800	35	25.44	18.96	6.48	35

Source: James B. Harper, *A Summary of Consumer Installment Credit Laws and Rules in The United States and Canada,* Morristown, N. J., 1968.

[a]Effective annual rate ceiling on loans with 12 month maturity, January 1, 1968.

[b]Range reflects grouping of states with the same yield.

Note: We are indebted to Helmuth Miller of Beneficial Finance Corporation for calculating these rates.

(43rd out of 47) for loans of $100, $200, and $300.

New York's loan ceiling of $800, as of the same date, was higher than that of 12 of the 47 states placing it below the median loan ceiling of $1,000. Yet neither the ranking nor the median reflects New York's real position since many states with low loan ceilings on their small loan law allow consumer finance companies to extend higher risk loans under other loan laws.[4] Taking these laws into account, New York's loan ceilings would rank 6th from the bottom.

Since the major function of consumer finance companies is to make higher-risk loans to borrowers who cannot meet any or all of their needs from lower-cost sources, their customers should represent a spectrum of credit risks ranging from those who cannot borrow else-

[4] These are often called industrial or instalment loan acts or discount acts.

where to those who need supplemental loans which are worth the premium in cost. Still others may borrow for reasons of convenience or privacy. As a lender of last resort, such companies will find themselves supplying small loans, say up to $500, although they might also supply larger loans to hard pressed borrowers who cannot borrow elsewhere. But the larger loan customers probably have greater ability to carry indebtedness and greater capacity to incur debt in larger amounts. Enacting a loan ceiling is a poor way to curtail borrowing of larger amounts unless the intent is to increase both the inconvenience and cost by making borrowers go to several credit sources. We shall present evidence to show that borrowing at more than one loan company is not uncommon while it is well known that borrowers patronize more than one type of credit agency when pressed for funds. For this reason, we do not believe that the loan ceiling is wholly effective as a deterrent to the growth of loans outstanding in New York except for those borrowers who would require more than two loans from licensed lenders where the custom among lenders is to deny loan requests when two loans already exist. Further, we believe that the rate ceiling has constrained the growth of licensed lending in New York first, because it is unusually low and second, because, as noted earlier, the trade-off between rate level, restricted entry, and risk impels us to draw the conclusion that New York's licensed lenders have no incentive to take the same risks if they are limited to lower rates of charge for loans and are protected from competition.

Comparison of Licensed Lending in New York With the U. S.

A comparison of licensed lending in New York with the nation's total personal loans – the aggregate of cash loans from commercial banks, sales finance companies, credit unions, consumer finance companies, and other financial institutions – reveals similar divergent growth rates.[5] As can be noted in Chart 2 or Table 4 licensed loans in New York represented only slightly less than 2 per cent of total personal loans in the U.S. in 1967, a percentage lower than any existing since the 1932 law was passed.

[5] Personal loans are defined by the Federal Reserve Board as including the aggregate of cash loans outstanding that are not specifically identified with the purchase of automobiles, other consumer durable goods, or home repair and modernization loans.

CHART 4

Net Bad Debt Charges in Per Cent of Average Oustanding Loans in New York, 1936-67

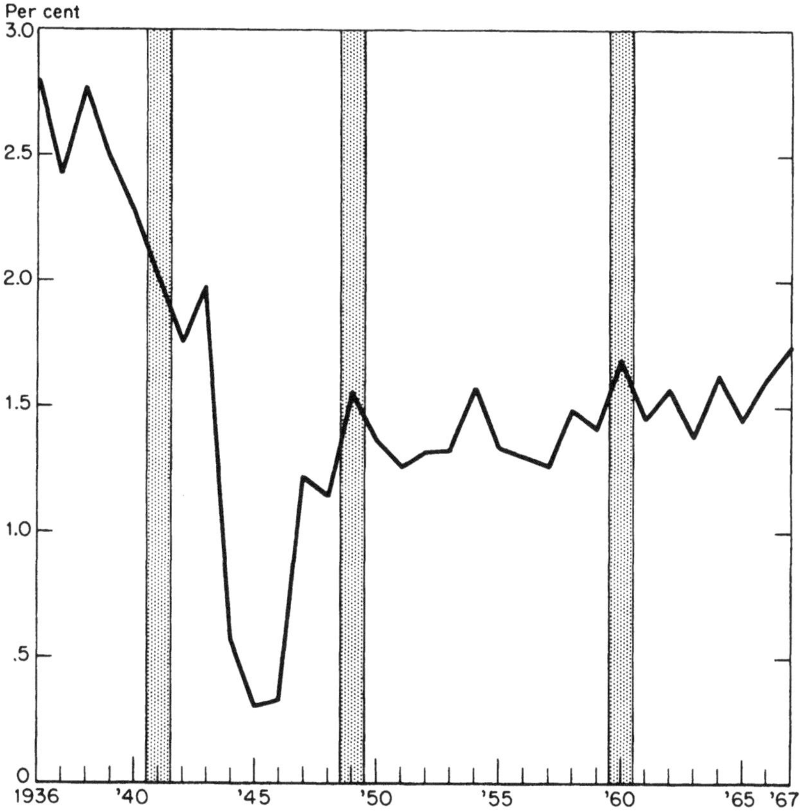

SOURCE: Table 6.

NOTE: Shading denotes years in which amendments were made in the New York law.

The declining trend in New York's share of the national market for personal loans should not be construed as an absolute decline in licensed lending in the state. End-of-year licensed loans outstanding increased at an average annual rate of $7.1 million between 1931 and

TABLE 6

Net Bad Debt Charges in Per Cent of Average Outstanding Loans in New York, 1936-67

Year	New York	Year	New York
1936	2.79	1952	1.32
1937	2.42	1953	1.32
1938	2.77	1954	1.58
1939	2.48	1955	1.33
1940	2.28	1956	1.30
1941	1.99	1957	1.26
1942	1.76	1958	1.49
1943	1.98	1959	1.41
1944	0.56	1960	1.69
1945	0.30	1961	1.45
1946	0.32	1962	1.57
1947	1.22	1963	1.38
1948	1.14	1964	1.63
1949	1.56	1965	1.44
1950	1.36	1966	1.61
1951	1.26	1967	1.73

Source: New York State Banking Department.

Note: Net bad debt charges equal charges to bad debts plus additions to reserve for bad debts less recoveries.

1940, $2.8 million between 1940 and 1948, $15.8 million between 1948 and 1959, and by $17.1 million between 1959 and 1967. If New York's licensed lending were not viewed in relation to other states, or to other financial institutions within the same state making personal loans, one would have to look further for signs that licensed loan services being generated in New York were not meeting the needs of all borrowers who have the capacity and willingness to repay their indebtedness.

The fact that absolute increases in licensed loans outstanding have occurred obscures the narrowing of the character of loan services provided in New York. Chart 4 and Table 6 reveal that net bad debt charges in New York have been held at relatively low levels since 1940, although the trend has been moderately rising in the last two decades. Also, the number of loans made under New York's small loan law has declined in four of the last nine years (Table 7). Further, the

TABLE 7

Number and Amount of Loans Made and Outstanding With Their Average 1959-67 Size in New York,

Year	No. of Loans Made During Year	Amount of Loans Made During Year (thousand dollars)	Average Size of Loans Made (dollars)	No. of Loans Outstanding at Year End	Amount of Loans Outstanding at Year End (thousand dollars)	Average Size of Loans Outstanding at Year End (dollars)
1959	1,101,354	413,069.4	375	868,389	268,377.1	309
1960	1,117,417	502,849.9	450	862,756	322,534.2	374
1961	919,198	457,782.4	498	840,929	331,369.0	394
1962	960,718	499,579.2	520	840,667	353,809.3	421
1963	945,940	505,634.0	535	847,894	367,946.5	434
1964	957,339	521,143.9	544	850,826	378,433.4	445
1965	975,803	541,784.8	555	866,496	395,778.6	457
1966	946,333	541,756.5	572	878,002	410,401.1	467
1967	877,105	517,847.4	590	854,854	404,896.9	474

Source: N.Y. State Banking Department.

Note: Dollar amounts for 1960 and subsequent years are net figures after excluding unearned interest charges resulting from precomputation.

number of loans made actually overstates the number of new borrowers since "double-ups" – multiple loans to a single borrower – cause the number of loans made (or outstanding) to a single borrower to be unknown. We shall present evidence in Chapter 5 to show the increased frequency of double-ups since September, 1957, when they were reported as comprising approximately 18 per cent of open accounts at licensed lenders' offices.[6] It is significant that the number of loans made have declined and the number of loans outstanding have remained roughly constant between 1959 and 1967 (Table 7).[7] The real gains in loans outstanding from licensed lenders have come

[6] *An Analysis of the Licensed Lender Industry, op. cit.*, p. 20.

[7] It is customary for some decrease in the number of loans made to occur after a change in loan ceiling, as in 1960, because there are fewer double-ups initially until the new ceiling again becomes restrictive.

from the increase in average size of loans made and outstanding (Table 7). A comment often heard from New York's licensed lenders is worth repeating here: "We are constantly making larger and larger loans to fewer and fewer borrowers in this state."

The year 1967 was the first recent year in which there was an actual decline in end-of-year loans outstanding from licensed lenders. 1967 was only the fifth year in which loans outstanding declined since 1914 and only the first year since the end of World War II to show a decrease. The decline was peculiar to New York and did not reflect general economic conditions in the nation. We view it likely that an increase in New Jersey's rate and loan ceiling adversely affected the number of borrowers served within the narrow spectrum of risk acceptable under the current statute in the state of New York. Other borrowers naturally graduate to lower-cost sources of credit (which is, of course, desirable) and these may not have been replaced by borrowers who previously could not qualify for loans in New York.

Growth of the Market for Personal Loans in New York, 1950-67

We have measured the amount of personal loans in New York statistically to approximate the Federal Reserve System's concept of personal loans as closely as possible. Thus, we included the F.D.I.C.'s reported estimates of commercial bank personal loans in New York, the New York State Banking Department's reported figures for savings bank policy loans, the Credit Union National Association's estimates of credit union receivables in New York,[8] and the licensed lenders' loans outstanding. The Credit Union figures contain some automobile financing that could not be removed so the growth of personal loans in New York is overstated. But the commercial bank, licensed lender, and savings bank data reflect closely the elements of personal loans that they are allowed to make under their New York statutes.

Chart 5 presents an index of the growth of the market for personal loans in New York for three of the four major institutional participants.[9] Table 8 presents the underlying data and, in addition, shows

[8] These data cover both federal-and state-chartered credit unions.

[9] The savings bank data were not shown on Chart 5, since the percentage growth rate would be misleading without consideration of the dollar amounts involved.

CHART 5

Index of Growth of End-of-Year Personal Loans Outstanding at Major Financial Institutions, 1950-67 (1950 = 100)

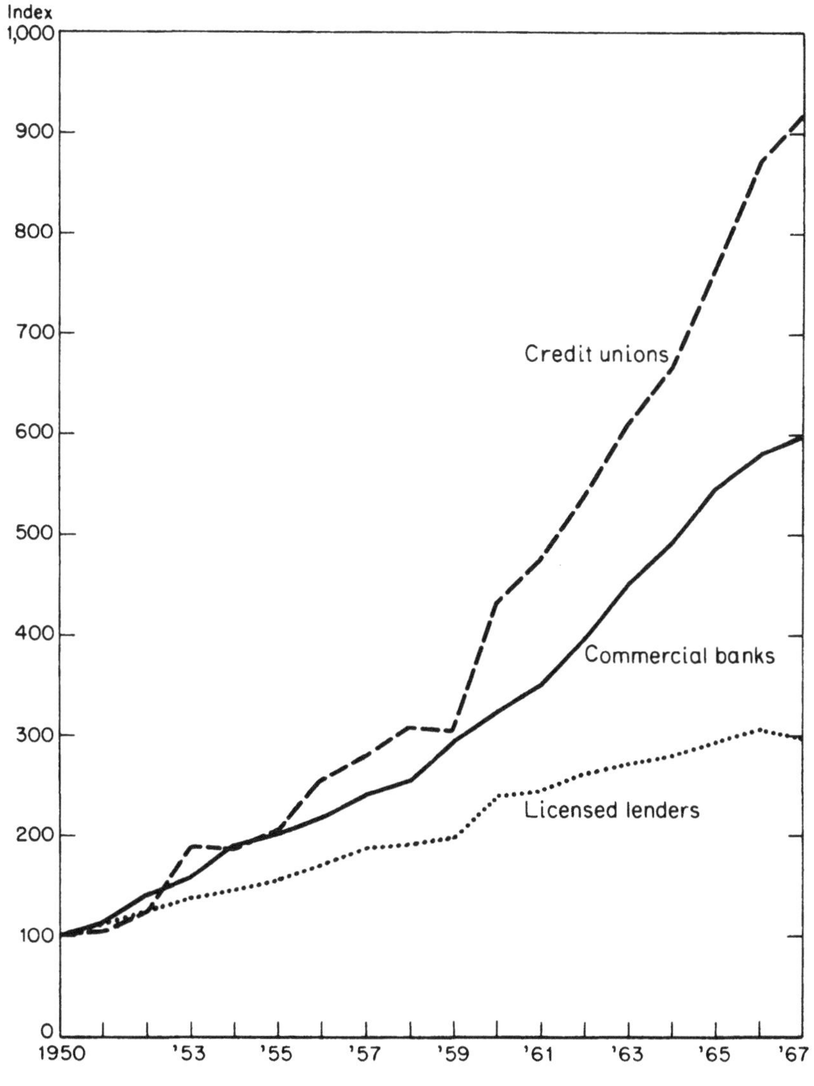

SOURCE: Table 8.

TABLE 8

Growth of the Market in End-of-Year Personal Loans Outstanding in New York and in the United States, 1950-67

(1950=100)

Year	N.Y. Licensed Lenders (1)	N.Y. Commercial Banks (2)	N.Y. Credit Unions (3)	N.Y. Savings Banks (4)
1950	100	100	100	100
1951	112	114	103	148
1952	124	141	124	123
1953	137	158	188	144
1954	146	191	185	292
1955	155	201	205	560
1956	170	217	255	991
1957	187	240	280	582
1958	191	253	308	960
1959	198	293	304	1,514
1960	238	322	434	1,757
1961	244	349	475	2,369
1962	261	396	538	2,139
1963	271	450	611	2,666
1964	279	492	666	3,384
1965	292	546	767	4,389
1966	305	580	871	5,355
1967	298	599	917	6,424
		Market Shares		
1950[a]	135,728(32)	245,929(57)	44,862(10)	3,091(1)
1967[a]	404,897(16)	1,472,576(59)	411,417(17)	198,572(8)

New York Total Personal Loans in Relation to the U.S. Market

	New York Total (5)	U.S. Regulated Small Loan Companies (6)	U.S. Total Personal Loans (7)
1950[b]	430,000(15)	1,195,000(42)	2,814,000(100)
1967[b]	2,487,000(10)	10,211,000(43)	24,018,000(100)

Source: col. 1, New York State Banking Department; col. 2, *Assets and Liabilities of Commercial Banks,* FDIC, "Other installment loans for personal expenditures"; col. 3, *International Credit Union Yearbook,* Credit Union National Association; col. 4, New York State Banking Department; col. 5, total of cols. 1, 2, 3, and 4; cols. 6 and 7, Board of Governors of the Federal Reserve System.

[a] Dollar amounts in thousands. Figures in parentheses are percentage of total personal loans in New York for that year.

[b] Dollar amounts in thousands. Figures in parentheses are percentage of total personal loans in the United States for that year.

the absolute dollar amounts and percentage shares of the market for the four institutional participants. Credit unions have shown the most rapid growth of the three institutional participants shown on Chart 5, but this growth undoubtedly reflects the inclusion of automobile financing. Commercial banks' personal loans increased sixfold despite exclusion of automobile and other financing during the sixteen year period, comparing favorably with the ninefold increase for credit unions, and the threefold increase in loans outstanding from licensed lenders. Mutual savings banks' passbook loan growth by 1967 was 64 times their 1950 outstandings, representing rapid growth from a low base in that year.

Commercial banks held the largest share of the market in 1950, 57 per cent, which increased to 59 per cent in 1967 (Table 8). Licensed lenders' market share dropped from 32 to 16 per cent, reflecting the smaller growth rate. Credit unions' market share rose from 10 to 17 per cent while mutual savings bank passbook loans outstanding grew from only 1 per cent to 8 per cent of the total. The performance of licensed lenders in New York ran counter to national trends. Regulated small loan companies' share of personal loans outstanding in the U.S. rose from 42 to 43 per cent while New York's share dropped from 15 to 10 per cent during the same period (Table 8).

Per Capita Average Personal Loans Outstanding in New York and in the U. S.

In order to correct for differences in the rate of growth in population between New York and the U.S., a better comparative measure of the divergent growth trend of personal loans in New York and in the U.S. will be per capita average loans outstanding. In Chart 6 and Table 9, we present comparisons of the average amount of loans out-

CHART 6

Per Capita Average Personal Loans Outstanding at Regulated Small Loan Companies, N.Y. and U.S., 1950-67

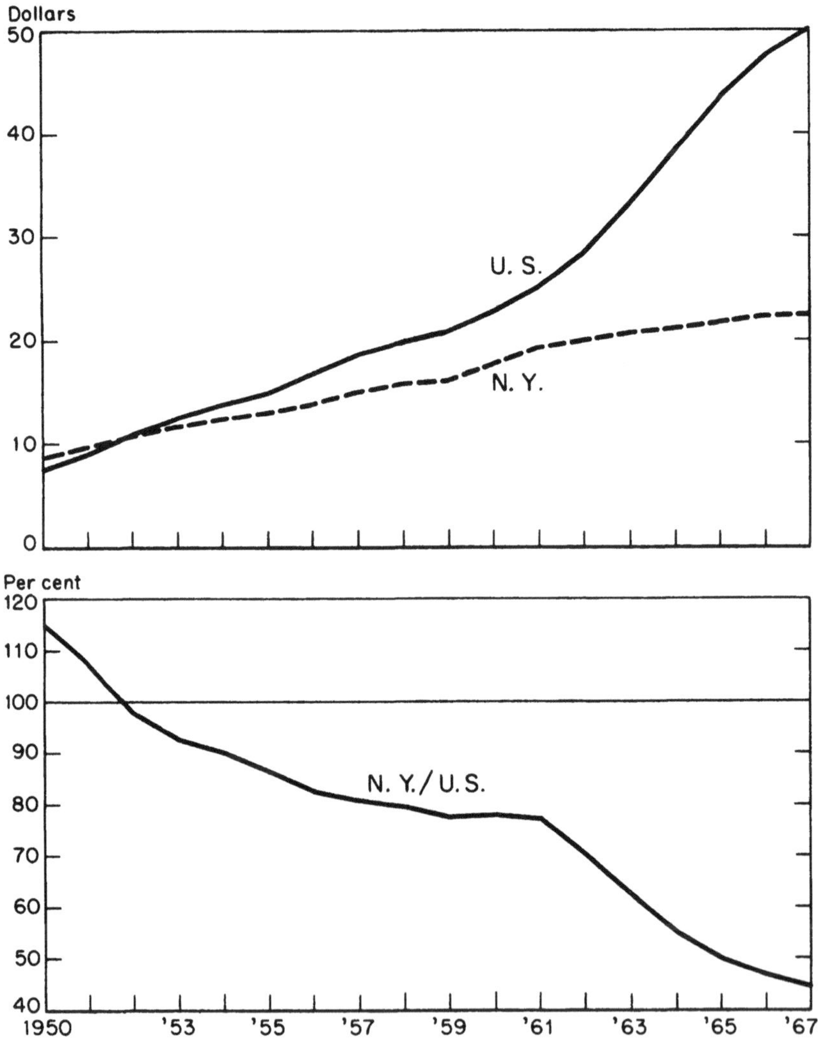

Source: Table 9.

TABLE 9

Per Capita Average Personal Loans Outstanding at Regulated Small Loan Companies, N.Y. and U.S., 1950-67

(dollars)

Year	N.Y. (1)	U.S. (2)	Col. 1 ÷ by Col. 2 (per cent) (3)
1950	8.51	7.40	115.0
1951	9.57	8.92	107.3
1952	10.61	10.84	97.9
1953	11.51	12.48	92.2
1954	12.30	13.66	90.0
1955	12.85	14.87	86.4
1956	13.72	16.64	82.5
1957	14.95	18.52	80.7
1958	15.57	19.58	79.5
1959	15.91	20.57	77.3
1960	17.59	22.59	77.9
1961	19.24	24.97	77.1
1962	19.83	28.26	70.2
1963	20.51	33.01	62.1
1964	20.96	38.22	54.8
1965	21.50	43.45	49.5
1966	22.14	47.43	46.7
1967	22.31	50.12	44.5

Source: Col. 1, N.Y. State Banking Department; Col. 2, Board of Governors of the Federal Reserve System.

standing per person during the year from licensed lenders in New York and per capita regulated personal loans outstanding in the United States. The upper panel of the chart reveals that licensed loans outstanding in New York were higher than the U.S. regulated personal loan average in 1950, but that the positions were reversed in the intervening years. New York fell below the U.S. average in 1952 and fell progressively farther behind until, in 1967, the New York average was less than half of the U.S. average. This is, indeed, a measure of the regulated personal loan gap in New York State.

CHART 7

Per Capita Average Personal Loans Outstanding from Commercial Banks, Credit Unions, and Mutual Savings Banks, N.Y. and U.S., 1950-67

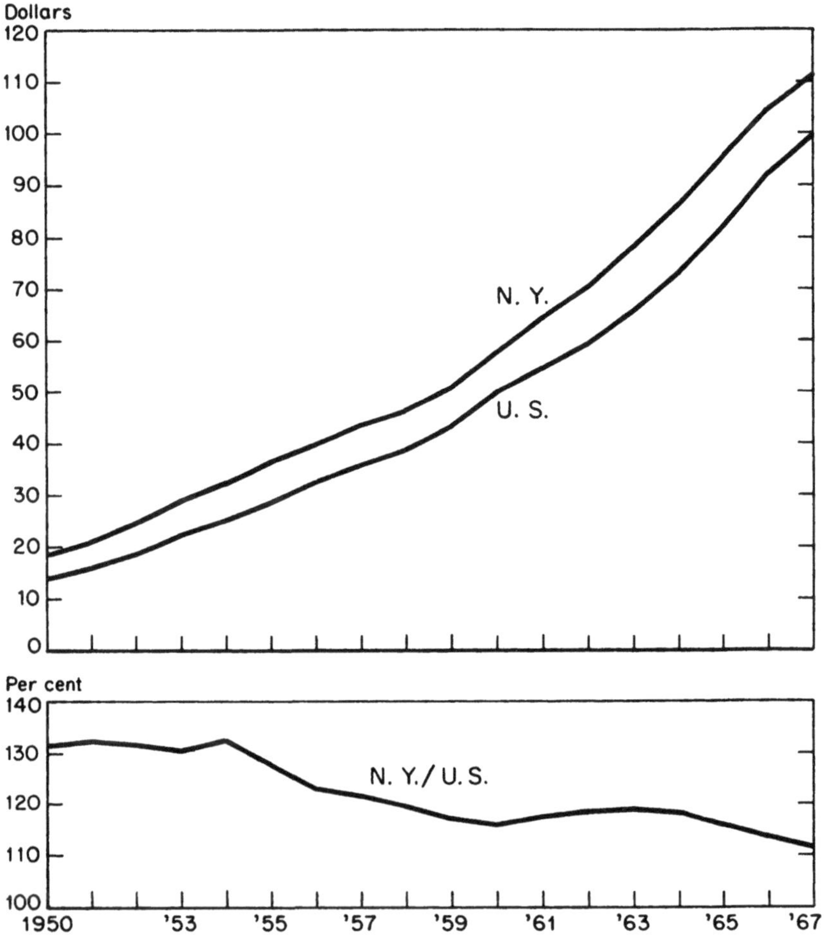

Source: Table 10.

TABLE 10

Per Capita Average Personal Loans Outstanding From Commercial Banks, Credit Unions, and Mutual Savings Banks, N.Y. and U.S., 1950-67

(dollars)

Year	U.S. (1)	N.Y. (2)	Col. 1 ÷ by Col. 2 (per cent) (3)
1950	13.90	18.25	131.3
1951	15.80	20.86	132.0
1952	18.46	24.28	131.5
1953	22.14	28.80	130.1
1954	25.09	32.20	132.3
1955	28.67	36.59	127.6
1956	32.65	39.99	122.5
1957	35.89	43.52	121.2
1958	38.67	46.19	119.4
1959	43.49	50.80	116.8
1960	50.07	57.94	115.7
1961	54.69	64.23	117.4
1962	59.14	70.05	118.4
1963	65.74	78.06	118.7
1964	73.09	86.44	118.3
1965	82.45	95.47	115.8
1966	92.55	104.90	113.3
1967	99.95	111.27	111.3

Source: Federal Deposit Insurance Corporation, Credit Union National Association, N.Y. State Banking Department, and Board of Governors of the Federal Reserve System.

It is apparent that other institutional sources of personal loans in New York have maintained their relative position much better than licensed lenders. Chart 7 and Table 10 reveal that per capita personal loans outstanding from the combined commercial banks, savings banks, and credit unions remain above their corresponding average nationally in the personal loan market. There has been a relative decline in their rates of growth but not nearly as severe as that experienced by licensed lenders in New York. For both groups, however, the data suggest that there has been faster growth of personal loans in the country as a whole than in New York.

Our statistical investigation of the licensed lending industry leads us to believe that the existence of a relatively low rate and loan ceiling structure have contributed to the low level and adverse growth trend of licensed loans in New York relative to consumer finance company personal loans in the U.S. Other sources of personal loans have grown more rapidly than licensed lenders and their personal loans outstanding from their counterparts in the U.S. But their relative growth trend has been declining, too. This declining growth trend may be due to more restrictive legislation in New York, which we have not investigated, or a more favorable climate for retail instalment financing causing less demand for loans. But these hypotheses cannot be tested with present statistics.[10]

[10] Retail instalment financing statistics cannot be broken down by states because data from sales finance companies have not been collected or published on this basis.

III

Trends in Operating Income and Expense of Licensed Lenders in New York

We have noted in the preceding chapters that the slower growth rate of licensed lending in New York has accompanied a regulatory point of view that such lending should be stabilized by more restrictive regulation commencing in 1941. Since that time, experience with the more restrictive rate ceilings has raised some fundamental questions which will be considered in the remaining chapters of this study. First, how has the financial status of the licensed lenders in New York fared under the existing regulatory philosophy since 1960? Has it been possible to maintain an environment which can encourage a sufficient number of firms to generate loans profitably within the restrictive confines of the small loan law and the limited opportunities for lending permitted by it? We have suggested that one way lenders have adjusted in the past was to limit their loan services to less risky borrowers, who do not require the more extensive investigation, servicing, and collection services that would necessitate the higher rates charged to borrowers in the rest of the country. But if the industry has made this adjustment in the past, can it continue to offset the effects of rising costs under the rate ceiling structure adopted in 1941 and amended slightly in 1949 and 1960? These questions will be examined in Chapters 3 and 4.

Other questions challenge the basic philosophy underlying the current regulation of licensed lending. How can restrictive rate and loan ceilings combat economic forces that indicate a demand for loan services that cannot be provided under the existing statute? To what extent does the current statute contribute to evasions of the intent of the law rather than to restrict borrowing within the stated limits? Are these evasions desirable or tolerable under current conditions? Do they suggest the need to reexamine the 1941 regulatory philosophy in the light of the economy of the late 1960's? These aspects of New York's experience will be considered in Chapter 5.

Composition of the Licensed Lending Industry in New York

The number of organizations holding licenses to make loans under the small loan law in New York State grew from 21 in 1931 to a peak of 75 in 1941. In 1945, there were 57 organizations holding licenses and the number grew again to a secondary peak of 74 organizations in 1955 and 1956. Since that time the number has declined to a total of 57 organizations operating under the small loan law at the end of 1967

TABLE 11

Number of Licensed Lending Organizations and Offices in New York State, 1931-67

Year	Number of Organizations	Number of Offices	Year	Number of Organizations	Offices
1931	21	n.a.	1950	62	314
1932	29	78	1951	60	328
1933	42	143	1952	60	335
1934	51	186	1953	67	356
1935	59	205	1954	73	385
1936	61	237	1955	74	408
1937	64	265	1956	74	433
1938	61	269	1957	64	441
1939	67	288	1958	64	450
1940	69	308	1959	64	465
1941	75	317	1960	61	470
1942	66	298	1961	59	475
1943	57	268	1962	59	485
1944	58	269	1963	56	494
1945	57	270	1964	57	502
1946	57	282	1965	54	511
1947	60	286	1966	54	518
1948	61	289	1967	57	549
1949	61	296			

Source: New York State Banking Department.
n.a.—not available.

The number of offices, however, has grown steadily in all but the wartime years since 1932. The increase in the number of offices in New York suggests a steady demand for new licenses under the Banking Department's policy of limiting the competition among offices for borrowers in a given area according to standards of convenience and advantage to a given locality. Between 1932 and 1967, the number of loan offices in New York State grew from 78 to 549.

The conflicting trend in the declining number of organizations and the rising number of offices suggests two observations. First, with fewer organizations competing within the state, there is less competitive pressure among firms than before. Second, fewer firms are providing a greater number of facilities, suggesting that there are still economic advantages to securing a license to operate in New York, and, in fact, good new locations are still sought after. Locations in New York City may be an exception since the number of offices remained virtually stable during 1965, 1966, and 1967.[1]

National chain organizations have long been important suppliers of small loans in New York State. In 1967, 16 such consumer finance companies held three-quarters of the licensed offices in New York, which represented 84 per cent of loans outstanding at year end (Table 12). Thirteen state chains held 17 per cent of the licenses, representing 11 per cent of loans outstanding, while the remaining 28 independent companies accounted for 8 per cent of the offices and 5 per cent of the year-end loans outstanding. Between 1959 and 1967 these proportions changed little, indicating that there has been little difference in the composition of the licensed lending industry in New York State when classed by type of organization.

We shall present data in this chapter from 16 of the 27 organizations holding licenses in New York State in 1967 that responded to our

[1] The number of licensed offices in New York City in the four year period 1964-67, inclusive, totaled 196, 198, 199, and 199. The corresponding numbers for the state as a whole totaled 502, 511, 518, and 549.

TABLE 12

Licensed Lending Offices in New York State by Organization Classification, 1959-67

(millions of dollars)

Year	National Chains				State Chains				Independents			
			End-of-Year Outstandings				End-of-Year Outstandings				End-of-Year Outstandings	
	Organ-izations	Offices	Amount	Per Cent	Organ-izations	Offices	Amount	Per Cent	Organ-izations	Offices	Amount	Per Cent
1959	16	339	213.0	81.9	13	76	32.5	12.5	35	48	14.8	5.6
1960	17	347	256.6	81.9	13	79	40.9	13.1	32	43	15.7	5.0
1961	16	350	264.7	81.8	13	82	42.8	13.2	31	41	16.0	5.0
1962	16	354	280.5	81.7	13	88	46.5	13.5	30	39	16.5	4.8
1963	16	360	291.3	81.1	13	95	50.5	14.1	28	37	17.2	4.8
1964	16	362	298.4	81.0	13	101	52.3	14.2	28	38	17.8	4.8
1965	14	373	321.4	81.2	12	97	54.6	13.8	28	39	19.7	5.0
1966	14	379	334.0	81.4	13	99	55.9	13.6	27	38	20.4	5.0
1967	16	413	338.7	83.7	13	93	45.5	11.2	28	43	20.7	5.1

Source: New York State Banking Department.

Note: 1967 data are end-of-year; 1959-66 data are as of September 30.

request for reports submitted to the Banking Department during the previous ten years. Firms that were not in operation in New York during the entire ten-year period were excluded from the sample along with some smaller firms that were not numerous enough to form a cohesive size group. The three size groups established consisted of very large, large, and medium-sized companies whose 1964 consumer finance receivables were $150 million or more, $10 million to $150 million, and from $500,000 to $10 million, respectively. Firms whose receivables were less than $500,000 did not respond in numbers large enough to include in the sample. The proportion of total offices held by each size category among the sixteen firms did not vary appreciably between 1959 and 1967 (Table 13).

We shall consider trends in income and expense ratios to average outstanding loans for (1) all licensees in New York State and (2) licensees in the three size groups from our sample, in order to ascertain any differences in the financial status of licensed lenders between 1960 and 1967. These trends will help determine whether the amendments to the small loan law in 1960 permitted the organizations in operation in New York to earn reasonable returns consistent with loan services rendered.

Income and Expense Ratios for All Licensees in New York State

GROSS INCOME RATIO TO AVERAGE LOANS OUTSTANDING

The average gross income ratio for New York State licensees increased from 20.6 per cent in 1960 to 21.2 per cent in 1961 as a result of the rate ceiling increase, loan ceiling increase, and the switch to precomputed interest allowed in the 1960 amendment to the law (Chart 8 and Table 14). After 1961, the ratio declined appreciably for two years, remained fairly stable for two years at about 20.0 per cent, and resumed a further decline after 1965 to a level of 19.6 per cent in 1967. Since most companies charge the ceiling rate in New York, decreases in the gross income ratio represent the less than proportional increase in income when the average size of loans outstanding increases. Chart 9 and Table 15 reveal the upward movement of the average

TABLE 13

Number and Proportion of Licensed Lending Offices Held by Size Groups Among Sample Companies in New York State, 1959-67

Year	Total Licensed Offices in New York State	Eight Very Large Companies		Four Large Companies		Four Medium-Sized Companies		Sample Per Cent of Total
		Offices	Per Cent of Total	Offices	Per Cent of Total	Offices	Per Cent of Total	
1959	465	289	62	30	6	12	3	71
1960	470	298	63	33	7	12	3	73
1961	475	300	63	36	8	12	2	73
1962	485	306	63	41	8	13	3	74
1963	494	310	63	42	8	14	3	74
1964	502	311	62	46	9	16	3	74
1965	511	320	63	46	9	16	3	75
1966	518	322	62	46	9	16	3	74
1967	549	336	61	40	7	16	3	71

Source: New York State Banking Department and Graduate School of Business of Columbia University.

CHART 8

Gross and Net Income, Before and After Interest and Taxes, as a Percentage of Average Loans Outstanding, New York State Totals, 1960-67

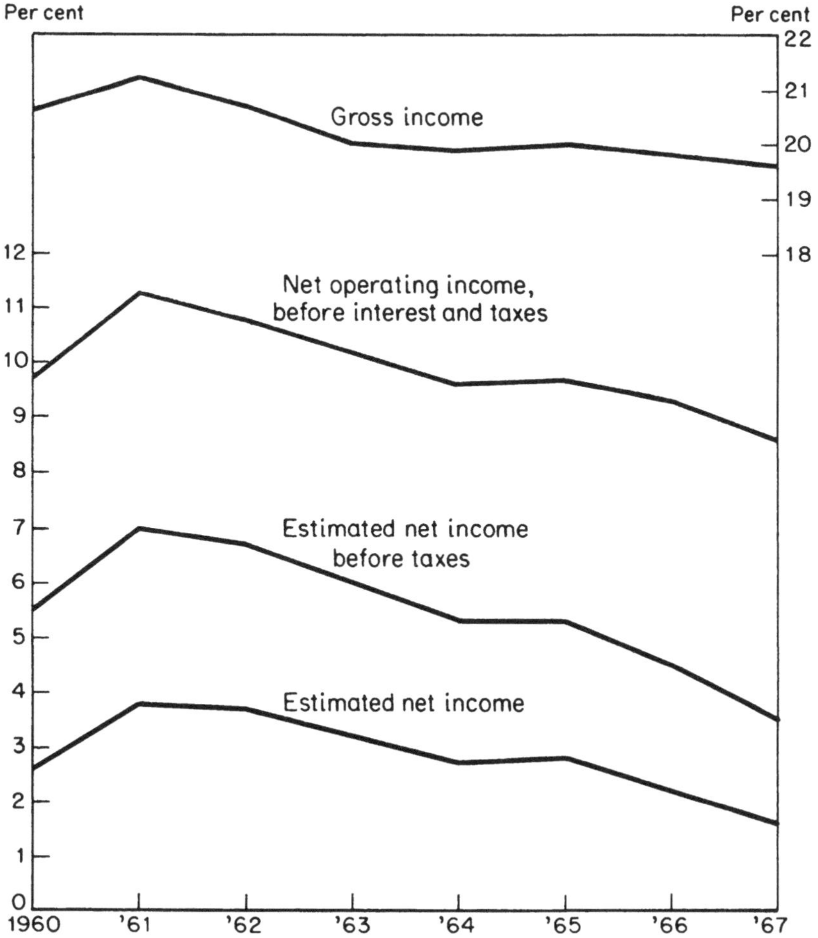

SOURCE: Table 14.

TABLE 14

Gross and Net Income, Before and After Interest and Taxes, as a Percentage of Average Loans Outstanding, New York State Totals, 1960-67

(amounts in thousands of dollars)

	1960		1961	1962	1963	1964	1965	1966	1967	
	Amount	Per Cent	Per Cent	Per Cent	Per Cent	Per Cent	Per Cent	Per Cent	Amount	Per Cent
Total operating income	60,805	20.6	21.2	20.7	20.0	19.9	20.0	19.8	80,008	19.6
Less: operating expense, including provision for bad debts	32,038	10.9	9.9	9.9	9.8	10.3	10.3	10.5	44,755	11.0
Net operating income before interest and taxes	28,767	9.7	11.3	10.8	10.2	9.6	9.7	9.3	35,253	8.6
Less: estimated interest expense	12,409	4.2	4.3	4.1	4.2	4.3	4.4	4.8	20,790	5.1
Estimated net income before taxes	16,359	5.5	7.0	6.7	6.0	5.3	5.3	4.5	14,465	3.5
Less: taxes, estimated federal and state	10,071	2.9	3.2	3.0	2.8	2.6	2.5	2.3	9,477	1.9
Estimated net income	6,287	2.6	3.8	3.7	3.2	2.7	2.8	2.2	4,986	1.6

Source: New York State Banking Department.

loan size from $341 in 1960 to $470 in 1967. As may be noted, the raising of the loan limit accompanied a sharp initial increase in average loan size in 1960 and 1961, which slowed down somewhat in the years which followed.

NET OPERATING INCOME RATIO, BEFORE INTEREST AND TAXES, TO AVERAGE LOANS OUTSTANDING

The net operating income ratio increased sharply in 1961, reflecting the increase in gross income and an accompanying decline in operating expense associated with the increase in average loan size when the loan ceiling was raised. Chart 8 and Table 14 reveal that after 1961, the net income ratio before interest and taxes declined more sharply than the gross income ratio reflecting the rise in the rate of operating expenses. Operating expense ratios, shown in Table 14, rose sharply after 1963, causing net operating income to decline in 1964 and 1965, and contributing to the sharper decline (with the decline in gross income ratios) in 1966 and 1967. Overall, the net operating income ratio declined from 9.7 per cent in 1960 to 8.6 per cent in 1967. Despite the initial favorable impact of the 1960 amendments to the small loan law, it appears that rising expenses and declining incomes have again reduced the margin of return on average loans outstanding below the 1960 level.[2]

ESTIMATED NET INCOME BEFORE TAXES

A major element decreasing the profits of licensed lenders during the 1960-67 period has been the rising costs of borrowed funds.

Analysis of net income before interest and taxes neglects an important cost, interest, over which licensed lenders have little control. Yet interest payments reported to the Banking Department are subject to the same inaccuracies that were noted earlier with respect to the reporting by interstate companies of capital and borrowed funds.[3] For this reason we found it necessary to estimate interest costs separately

[2] Since the law went into effect in mid-1960, the 1960 ratios do not portray pre-amendment conditions.

[3] See above, Chapter I, note 44.

CHART 9

Comparison of Average Loan Size with Loan Limit in New York State, 1951-67

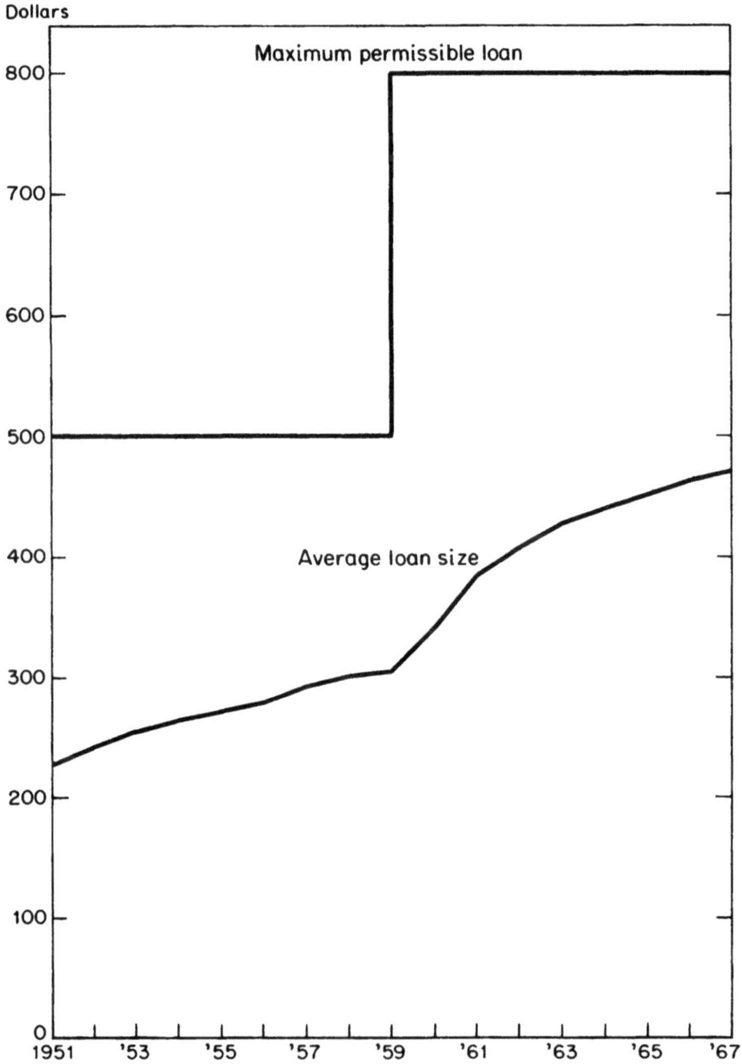

SOURCE: Table 15.

TABLE 15
Comparison of Average Loan Size With Loan Limit in New York State, 1951-67
(dollars)

Year	Maximum Permissible Loan	Average Loan Size
1951	500	228
1952	500	242
1953	500	255
1954	500	263
1955	500	269
1956	500	279
1957	500	292
1958	500	300
1959	500	305
1960	800	341
1961	800	384
1962	800	407
1963	800	427
1964	800	439
1965	800	451
1966	800	462
1967	800	470

Source: New York State Banking Department.

for companies whose operations were not confined entirely to New York.[4] By deducting estimated interest costs for interstate companies and reported interest costs for intrastate companies from net income before interest and taxes, we arrived at our estimates of net income before taxes.

[4] Licensed lenders in New York have an option in their method of reporting the source and cost of their loanable funds. Some companies report them as borrowed funds while others list them as allocated Branch Office Capital. To insure uniformity of treatment, all interstate companies were handled in an identical manner. It seems reasonable to assume that borrowing costs per dollar of borrowed funds are similar for interstate companies of a given size category no matter in which state the funds are used. This is a result of their borrowing power and their ability to obtain funds from a wide range of institutional sources.

The procedure for estimating interest expense is as follows: interest expense as a percentage of average personal loans outstanding is determined nationally for each of seven size groups from the sample of companies reporting data to the National Consumer Finance Association. Then the companies in the corresponding

Estimated net income before taxes rose from 5.5 per cent in 1960 to 7.0 per cent in 1961 because estimated interest expense stayed about the same and net income before interest and taxes rose sharply (Chart 8 and Table 14). After 1962, interest expense estimates rose steadily, rising sharply in 1966 and 1967. The increased interest costs caused estimated net income before taxes to decline severely, from 5.5 per cent in 1960 to 3.5 per cent in 1967. This decline of 2.0 percentage points over the period is almost twice the 1.1 percentage point decline in net income before interest and taxes. By 1967, estimated interest expense represented 26 per cent of gross income. In 1960, the corresponding figure was only 20 per cent.

ESTIMATED NET INCOME RATIOS

Net income ratios to average loans outstanding result from deducting estimated tax expense from net income before taxes.[5] The decline in estimated net income ratios after taxes was more moderate than the decline in estimated net income before taxes between 1960 and 1967. Estimated net income ratios to average loans outstanding declined on average for all licensees, from 2.6 per cent in 1960 to 1.6 per cent in 1967. The financial status of licensed lenders deteriorated most seriously during 1966 and 1967 when the impact of rising money costs accentuated the more gradual deterioration of net profits on outstand-

size groups in New York are allocated interest expense according to the NCFA size group's percentage of their average personal loans outstanding. This rate is then applied to the company's average personal loans outstanding reported in New York. This procedure is followed only for interstate companies; interest expense percentages for intrastate companies is based on company reports. The company interest expense estimates are then combined into the size groups used in this chapter: very large, large and medium-sized companies. At first, this procedure may appear somewhat artificial; however, the diverse reporting employed by these companies make it impossible to obtain reasonably homogeneous interest expense data for them. Therefore, interest expense figures for these offices have been derived on the basis of the previously mentioned national norm.

[5] Tax expense is estimated in a manner similar to interest expense for similar reasons. Federal taxes for interstate companies are national expenses. It therefore appears logical to allocate them to New York in the same proportion of average personal loans outstanding in the state as is the case nationally according to the NCFA. This procedure is followed only for federal taxes and only for interstate companies. Reported state taxes are added to estimated federal taxes and subtracted from net income before taxes to obtain net income.

ing loans which has occurred regularly since 1941.[6]

Comparability of Data From Sample of Licensed Lenders With That for Total New York State Licensees

Before turning to the operating experience of licensed lenders classified by company size, we shall examine the comparability of our sample data with that obtained from all licensees by the New York State Banking Department. It can be recalled that the sample consists of eight very large companies, four large companies, and four medium-sized companies, excluding those companies whose 1964 consumer finance receivables were below $500,000.[7]

Examination of Chart 10 and Table 16 reveals that movements of sample data correspond closely to movements of data reported by all licensees. The principal effect of relying upon sample data instead of the state totals is to exclude companies whose operations appear to be less profitable, as indicated by the higher net operating income ratios before interest and taxes for sample companies than for New York State licensees. The close comparability of these series gives us confidence that conclusions drawn from sample data will be fairly representative of the experience of all licensees in New York State.

Trends in Income and Expense Ratios by Size Groups in 1960-67

GROSS INCOME RATIOS

The behavior of the very large size group's gross income ratios

[6] This statement can be documented specifically by reference to the 1946 and 1957 Reports of the New York State Banking Department as reported above in Chapter I, notes 23 and 39.

[7] Companies of very large size are those with consumer finance receivables (as opposed to sales finance receivables) of $150,000,000 and up nationally, as determined by the NCFA.

Companies of large size are those with consumer finance receivables of $10,000,000 to $150,000,000 nationally.

Medium-sized companies are those with consumer finance receivables of $500,000 to $10,000,000 nationally.

Companies whose receivables were less than $500,000 reporting data for the entire 1960-1967 period were too few and too varied to represent the group.

CHART 10

Gross and Net Income, Before and After Interest and Taxes, as a Percentage of Average Loans Outstanding, Comparability of Sample Companies and New York State Totals, 1960-67

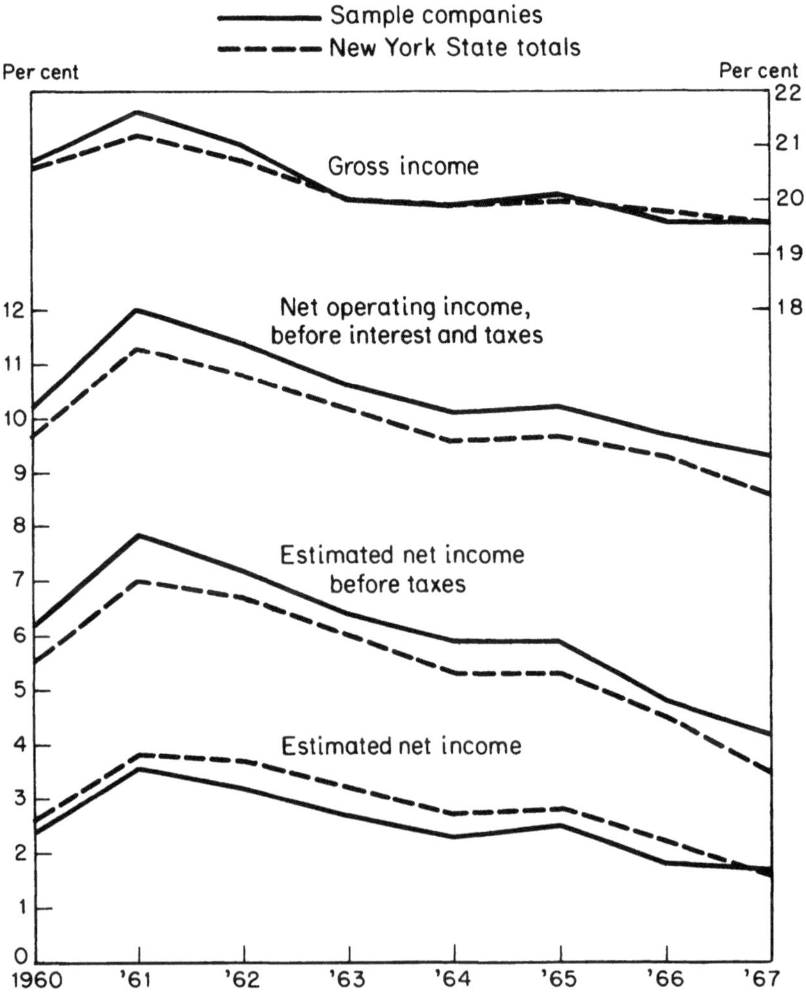

SOURCE: Table 16.

TABLE 16

Gross and Net Income, Before and After Interest and Taxes, as a Percentage of Average Loans Outstanding, Comparability of Sample Companies and New York State Totals, 1960-67

(amounts in thousands of dollars)

		1960		1961	1962	1963	1964	1965	1966	1967	
		Amount	Per Cent	Per Cent	Per Cent	Per Cent	Per Cent	Per Cent	Per Cent	Amount	Per Cent
Total operating income	Sample	49,260	20.7	21.6	21.0	20.0	19.9	20.1	19.6	65,853	19.6
	NYST	60,805	20.6	21.2	20.7	20.0	19.9	20.0	19.8	80,008	19.6
Less: operating expense including provision for bad debts	Sample	24,930	10.5	9.6	9.6	9.4	9.8	9.9	9.9	34,712	10.3
	NYST	32,038	10.9	9.9	9.9	9.8	10.3	10.3	10.5	44,755	11.0
Net operating income before interest and taxes	Sample	24,330	10.2	12.0	11.4	10.6	10.1	10.2	9.7	31,141	9.3
	NYST	28,767	9.7	11.3	10.8	10.2	9.6	9.7	9.3	35,253	8.6
Less: estimated interest expense	Sample	9,679	4.1	4.2	4.1	4.2	4.2	4.4	4.8	16,972	5.0
	NYST	12,409	4.2	4.3	4.1	4.2	4.3	4.4	4.8	20,790	5.1
Estimated net income before taxes	Sample	14,651	6.2	7.8	7.2	6.4	5.9	5.9	4.8	14,169	4.2
	NYST	16,359	5.5	7.0	6.7	6.0	5.3	5.3	4.5	14,463	3.5
Less: taxes, estimated federal and state	Sample	9,008	3.8	4.2	4.1	3.7	3.5	3.4	3.0	8,359	2.5
	NYST	10,071	2.9	3.2	2.9	2.8	2.6	2.5	2.3	9,477	1.9
Estimated net income	Sample	5,643	2.4	3.6	3.2	2.7	2.3	2.5	1.8	5,810	1.7
	NYST	6,287	2.6	3.8	3.7	3.2	2.7	2.8	2.2	4,986	1.6

Source: New York State Banking Department (state totals) and New York State Consumer Finance Association (sample).
Note: NYST denotes New York State totals.

shown in Chart 11 is similar to that for all licensees in the state, as might be expected since the very large companies hold a large proportion of outstanding loans in the state (72 per cent at the end of 1967). Among the three size groups, however, the decline in gross income ratios of 1.0 percentage point for the very large companies was intermediate between a –3.1 percentage point change in the large company group and a –.4 percentage point change in the medium-sized company category (Charts 11, 12, and 13; Tables 17, 18, and 19). Thus, the different movements of gross income ratios among the three groups are not patterned according to size. Within the large company group, the major exception, one company's experience tended to determine that group's wider swings in both the income and expense ratios during the period.

The general downward movement in gross income ratios for all licensees was reflected to varying degrees among the size groups in the sample.

NET OPERATING INCOME RATIOS BEFORE INTEREST AND TAXES

Operating expenses, including changes in the provision for bad debts, determine whether movement in gross income ratios affect net operating income before interest and taxes. As may be noted in Tables 17, 18, and 19, operating expense ratios decreased from 1960 to 1962 because of the large increases in average loans outstanding following the 1960 amendment to the law. After 1962, operating expense ratios rose gradually until, by 1967, they were in the neighborhood of the 1960 level. Operating expense ratios for companies in the large size group decreased by .7 of a percentage point between 1960 and 1967 while the very large company group's ratio decreased by only .1 percentage point. The medium-sized company group's operating expense ratio increased by .2 percentage points over the entire period.

Despite the decline in operating expense ratios over the 1960-67 period, the large company group suffered the largest drop in net income before interest and taxes – from 7.2 to 4.8 per cent (Table 18). The smallest decline from 8.7 to 8.1 per cent was experienced by the medium-sized companies, simply because they maintained their gross income levels while operating expenses rose only modestly (Table 19). The very large company group maintained the highest net operating income ratio of the three groups but experienced a decline from 10.6

CHART 11

Gross and Net Income, Before and After Interest and Taxes, as a Percentage of Average Loans Outstanding, Very Large Companies, 1960-67

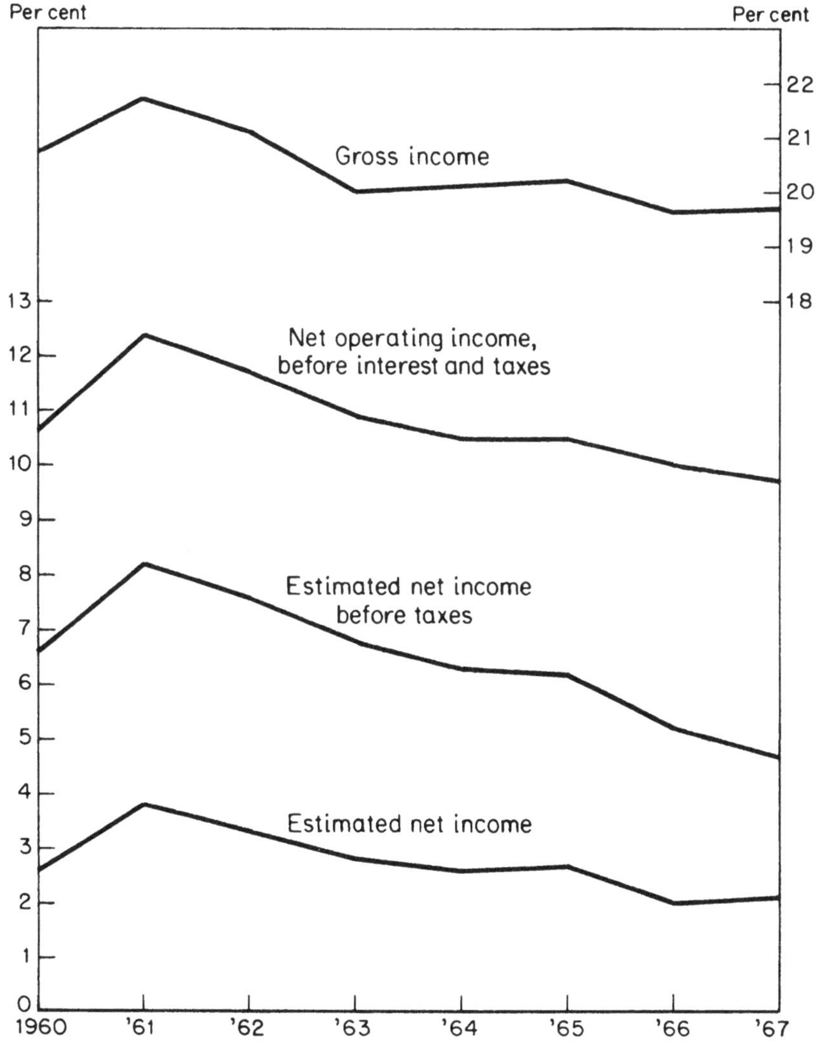

SOURCE: Table 17.

CHART 12

Gross and Net Income, Before and After Interest and Taxes, as a Percentage of Average Loans Outstanding, Large Companies, 1960-67

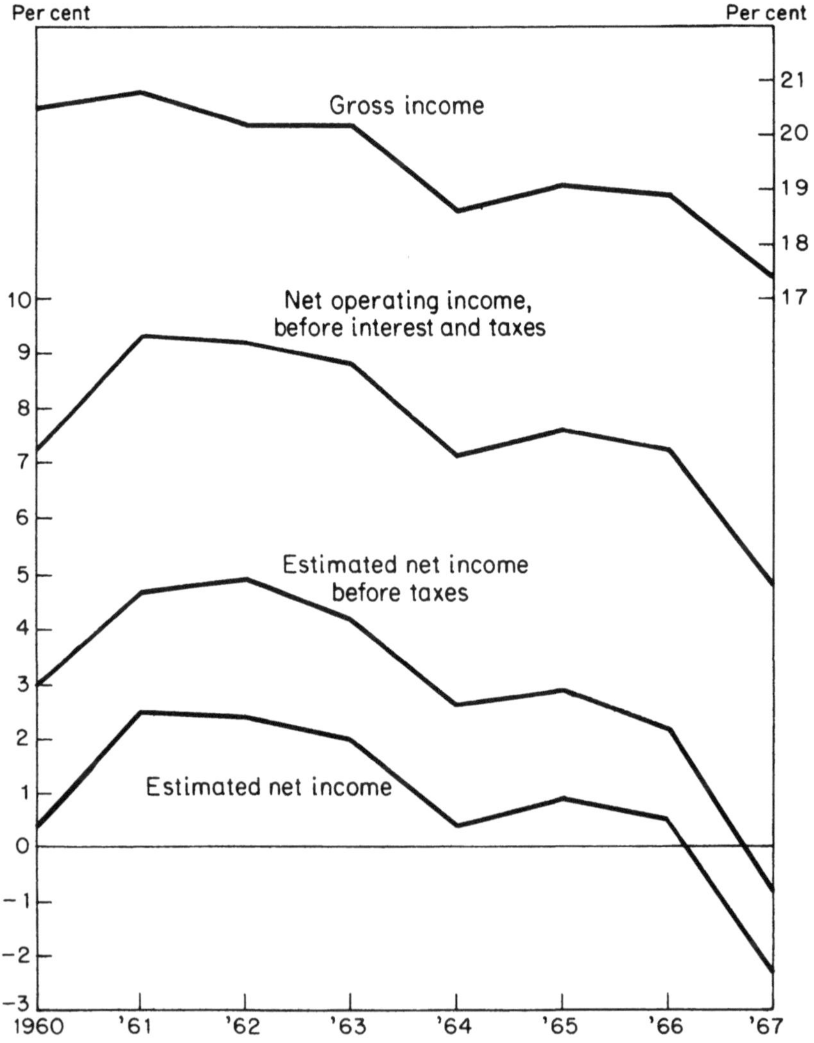

SOURCE: Table 18.

CHART 13

Gross and Net Income, Before and After Interest and Taxes, as a Percentage of Average Loans Outstanding, Medium-Sized Companies, 1960-67

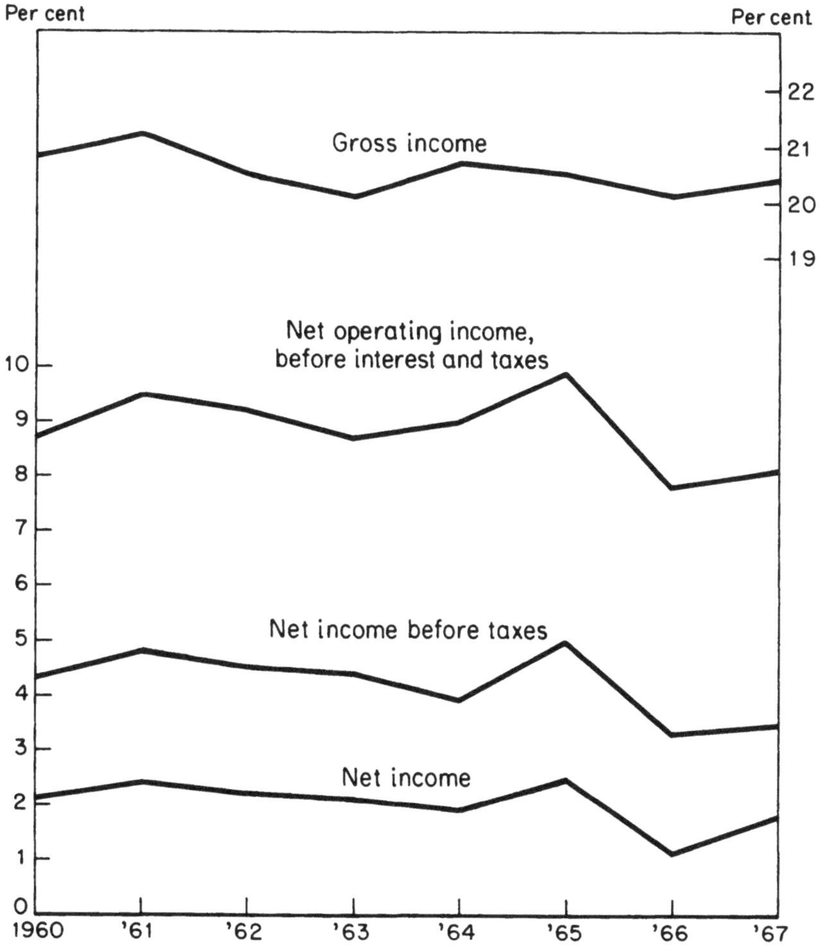

Source: Table 19.

TABLE 17

Gross and Net Income, Before and After Interest and Taxes, as a Percentage of Average Loans Outstanding, Very Large Companies, 1960-67

(amounts in thousands of dollars)

	1960		1961	1962	1963	1964	1965	1966	1967	
	Amount	Per Cent	Per Cent	Per Cent	Per Cent	Per Cent	Per Cent	Per Cent	Amount	Per Cent
Total operating income	43,441	20.7	21.7	21.1	20.0	20.1	20.2	19.6	59,028	19.7
Less: operating expense, including provision for bad debts	21,222	10.1	9.3	9.4	9.1	9.6	9.7	9.6	29,939	10.0
Net operating income before interest and taxes	22,219	10.6	12.4	11.7	10.9	10.5	10.5	10.0	29,089	9.7
Less: estimated interest expense	8,394	4.0	4.2	4.1	4.1	4.2	4.3	4.8	14,937	5.0
Estimated net income before taxes	13,825	6.6	8.2	7.6	6.8	6.3	6.2	5.2	14,152	4.7
Less: taxes, estimated federal and state	8,375	4.0	4.4	4.3	4.0	3.7	3.5	3.2	7,791	2.6
Estimated net income	5,450	2.6	3.8	3.3	2.8	2.6	2.7	2.0	6,361	2.1

Source: New York State Consumer Finance Association.

TABLE 18

Gross and Net Income, Before and After Interest and Taxes, as a Percentage of Average Loans Outstanding, Large Companies, 1960-67

(amounts in thousands of dollars)

	1960		1961	1962	1963	1964	1965	1966	1967	
	Amount	Per Cent	Per Cent	Per Cent	Per Cent	Per Cent	Per Cent	Per Cent	Amount	Per Cent
Total operating income	4,756	20.5	20.8	20.2	20.2	18.6	19.1	18.9	5,268	17.4
Less: operating expense, including provision for bad debts	3,089	13.3	11.5	11.0	11.4	11.5	11.5	11.7	3,834	12.6
Net operating income before interest and taxes	1,667	7.2	9.3	9.2	8.8	7.1	7.6	7.2	1,434	4.8
Less: estimated interest expense	1,062	4.6	4.6	4.3	4.6	4.5	4.7	5.0	1,684	5.6
Estimated net income before taxes	605	3.0	4.7	4.9	4.2	2.6	2.9	2.2	–250	–.8
Less: taxes, estimated federal and state	520	2.2	2.3	2.4	2.2	2.2	2.1	1.7	442	1.5
Estimated net income	85	.4	2.5	2.4	2.0	.4	.9	.5	–692	–2.3

Source: New York State Consumer Finance Association.

TABLE 19

Gross and Net Income, Before and After Interest and Taxes, as a Percentage of Average Loans Outstanding, Medium-Sized Companies, 1960-67

(Amounts in thousands of dollars)

	1960		1961	1962	1963	1964	1965	1966	1967	
	Amount	Per Cent	Per Cent	Per Cent	Per Cent	Per Cent	Per Cent	Per Cent	Amount	Per Cent
Total operating income	1,063	20.8	21.2	20.5	20.1	20.7	20.5	20.1	1,557	20.4
Less: operating expense, including provision for bad debts	619	12.1	11.7	11.3	11.4	11.7	10.6	12.3	939	12.3
Net operating income before interest and taxes	444	8.7	9.5	9.2	8.7	9.0	9.9	7.8	618	8.1
Less: estimated interest expense	223	4.4	4.7	4.7	4.3	5.1	4.9	4.5	351	4.6
Estimated net income before taxes	221	4.3	4.8	4.5	4.4	3.9	5.0	3.3	267	3.5
Less: taxes, estimated federal and state	113	2.2	2.4	2.3	2.3	2.0	2.5	2.2	126	1.7
Estimated net income	108	2.1	2.4	2.2	2.1	1.9	2.5	1.1	141	1.8

Source: New York State Consumer Finance Association.

per cent in 1960 to 9.7 per cent in 1967 (Table 17). Again, it is interesting to note that neither the levels of net operating income ratios nor their changes over the period were ordered according to the size categories.

ESTIMATED NET INCOME RATIOS BEFORE TAXES

Initially, we consider the effects of interest costs upon estimated net income before taxes among companies in our three size groups. As noted earlier, rising interest costs were a major factor in the decline in estimated net income ratios before taxes for all licensees in New York. The estimates of increased interest costs shown in Tables 17, 18, and 19 were 1.0 per cent for companies in the very large and large size groups between 1960 and 1967 (from 4.0 to 5.0 and 4.6 to 5.0 per cent, respectively) and considerably less for the medium-sized companies (from 4.4 to 4.6 per cent). Changes in interest rates and changes in the proportions of funds from the various sources of debt financing are the primary factors contributing to the observed shifts in estimated interest expense as a ratio to average loans outstanding.

As a result of changing interest costs, the estimated net income ratios before taxes of the very large and medium-sized companies declined to 4.7 and 3.5 per cent in 1967, compared to 6.6 and 4.3 per cent in 1960 (Charts 11 and 13). The estimated net income ratios for the large company group declined seriously from 3.0 per cent to a loss of –.8 per cent during the same period (Chart 12). Again, we must caution against accepting the average as representing the experience of all four companies in the large size group because the adverse experience of one company affected the group's performance.[8]

In Chart 14 and Table 20, possible sources of the difference in net income before taxes can be examined. In the top panel of Chart 14, it can readily be observed that the advantage the very large companies had over large companies in estimated interest costs in 1960 was maintained during the period. Meanwhile, the medium-sized companies interest costs rose less during the period, giving them a positive advantage over both of the larger size groups by 1967.

The movement of estimated net income ratios before taxes was

[8] Of the four companies, three showed profits after estimates of interest expenses were deducted.

CHART 14
Interest, Salary, and Bad Debt Expense as a Percentage of Average Loans Outstanding, 1960-67

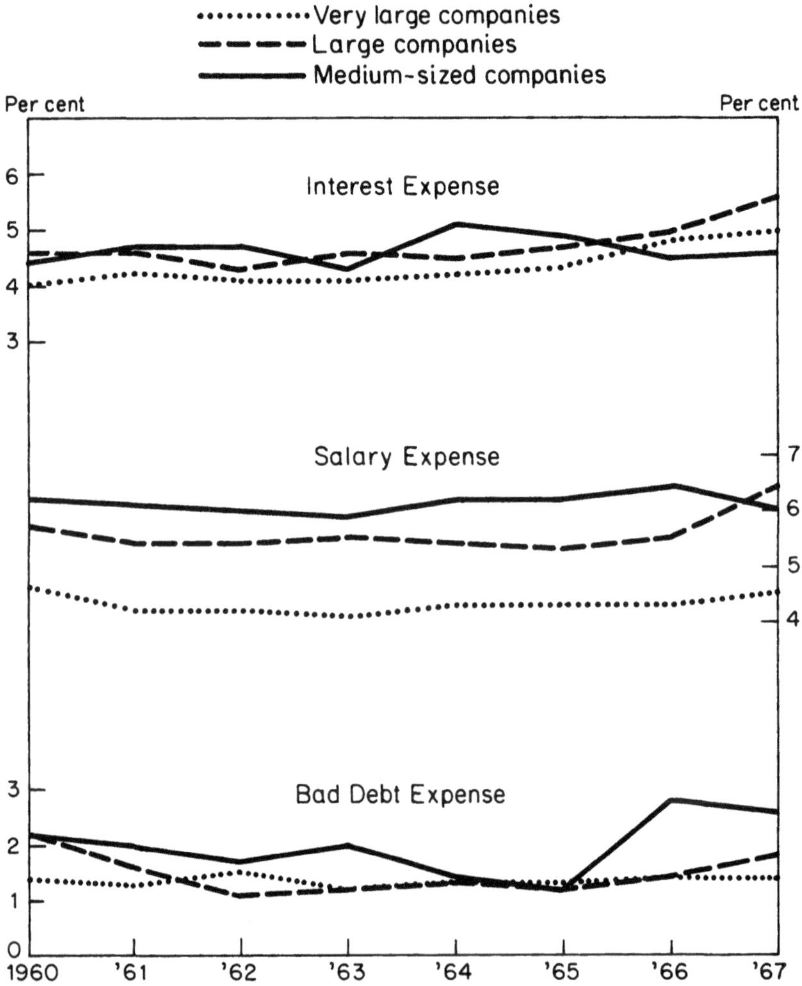

Source: Table 20.

TABLE 20
Interest, Salary, and Bad Debt Expense as a Percentage of Average Loans Outstanding, 1960-67

	1960	1961	1962	1963	1964	1965	1966	1967
A. Estimated Interest Expense								
Very large companies	4.0	4.2	4.1	4.1	4.2	4.3	4.8	5.0
Large companies	4.6	4.6	4.3	4.6	4.5	4.7	5.0	5.6
Medium-sized companies	4.4	4.7	4.7	4.3	5.1	4.9	4.5	4.6
B. Salary Expense								
Very large companies	4.6	4.2	4.2	4.1	4.3	4.3	4.3	4.5
Large companies	5.7	5.4	5.4	5.5	5.4	5.3	5.5	6.4
Medium-sized companies	6.2	6.1	6.0	5.9	6.2	6.2	6.4	6.0
C. Net Bad Debt Charge								
Very large companies	1.4	1.3	1.5	1.2	1.3	1.3	1.4	1.4
Large companies	2.2	1.6	1.1	1.2	1.3	1.2	1.4	1.8
Medium-sized companies	2.2	2.0	1.7	2.0	1.4	1.2	2.8	2.6

Source: New York State Consumer Finance Association.

also affected by other expenses. In the middle panel of Chart 14, it is apparent that the very large companies maintained a positive advantage in salary costs in per cent of average loans outstanding during the entire period, followed by the large size company group, while the medium-sized company group operated at a consistent disadvantage. The salary expense ratio reflects the dollar amounts of outstanding loans per employee as well as wage rates paid to employees. Thus, the utilization of employees' services, which, in turn, is related to the demand for loans in a given office location and the average size of loans handled, determines the competitive advantage or disadvantage attained by this measure. But this measure should not be used by itself to measure efficiency without consideration of the gross income ratio.

Under a graduated rate structure, the most costly loans to handle are the smaller loans, which, in turn, bring in a greater revenue to offset, in whole or in part, the extra expense.

The bottom panel of Chart 14 permits a comparison of bad debt ratios for the three company size groups. It is apparent that the medium-sized companies, the smallest size group shown, carried the highest bad debt ratios at a relatively high level through most of the period. It is likely, therefore, that only the adverse bad debt experience indicated in 1966 and 1967 greatly affected their net income before interest and taxes. In Chapter 4, we shall further consider expense items in per cent of income rather than in per cent of average loans outstanding in order to analyze the effects of these ratios upon profitability.

As of now, it is possible to state that the very large companies managed to maintain the highest ratios of estimated net income before taxes during the 1960-67 period but they, too, suffered sharply declining ratios from rising interest costs and the combination of rising operating expense ratios with declining gross income ratios. For these companies, as well as the other companies that fared more adversely during the 1960-67 period, operating experience in New York reflected declining profitability under restrictive rate and loan ceilings.

ESTIMATED NET INCOME RATIOS AFTER TAXES

Estimates of taxes may not be representative of taxes actually paid when the average for a group of interstate companies does not conform to the experience of the particular group of companies whose taxes are estimated. Interest costs are subject to the same kind of estimating error. Yet there is little doubt in our minds that the estimates we made represent the actual interest and taxes paid better than the allocations reported to the Banking Department by interstate companies.

Among the size groups, estimates of taxes paid seem reasonable for the very large and medium company size groups but may not represent the large size group because of the adverse experience of one company, which placed that group's before-tax net income sharply lower than the other two size groups and probably well below that group's national average, which formed the basis of the tax estimate.

Given the above qualification, we note in Tables 17 and 19 that estimated net income ratios after taxes declined from 2.6 to 2.1 per cent of average loans outstanding for very large companies and from 2.1 to 1.8 per cent for medium-sized companies in New York between 1960 and 1967. As was the case with the other income ratios, the decline followed an initial increase in net income in 1961. For the large company group, net income ratios after taxes dropped from 0.4 to −2.3 per cent between 1960 and 1967. The negative figure is indicative of overstatement of the group's tax liabilities, attributable again to the below-par record of one of the four companies in 1967.

Estimated Return on Average Total Assets and Capital, 1960-67

The behavior of the return on assets earned by licensed lenders, measured by estimated net income after interest and before taxes as a per cent of average total assets, is similar to the return shown as a per cent of average loans outstanding. Chart 15 portrays a rise from 5.3 per cent in 1960 to 6.8 per cent in 1961 and then a steady decline, except in 1965, to 3.3 per cent (Chart 15 and Table 21). We have chosen the return on assets, before taxes, as the best indication of the margin of profit earned, since it allows interest costs to be counted as an expense.[9] It is apparent from these data that the profitability of licensed lending was substantially improved for the first three calendar years after the 1960 change in the small loan law. But thereafter, any net gain was eroded by rising costs, so that the profitability of licensed lending slipped appreciably below the 1960 level.

But what of the incentive to attract capital? Again, this must be measured implicitly rather than directly, because of the poor quality of reported information. We have greater confidence in the measure to reflect changes, rather than the level of return to equity, during the period. As our measure, we present the estimated return, after taxes, on estimated average capital accounts of licensed lenders in New York (Chart 15 and Table 21). These estimates are similar in design but represent improvements on the estimates presented in the Chapman and Jones study and accepted by the Banking Department

[9] An alternate measure of "assets used and useful" estimated each year by Haskins and Sells for the New York State Consumer Finance Association would show still lower rates of return and strengthens the argument for adjustment of the small loan law at this time, if the rate base measure were accepted.

CHART 15
Estimated Return on Average Assets and Capital Under New York's Small Loan Law, All Licensees, State Totals, 1960-67

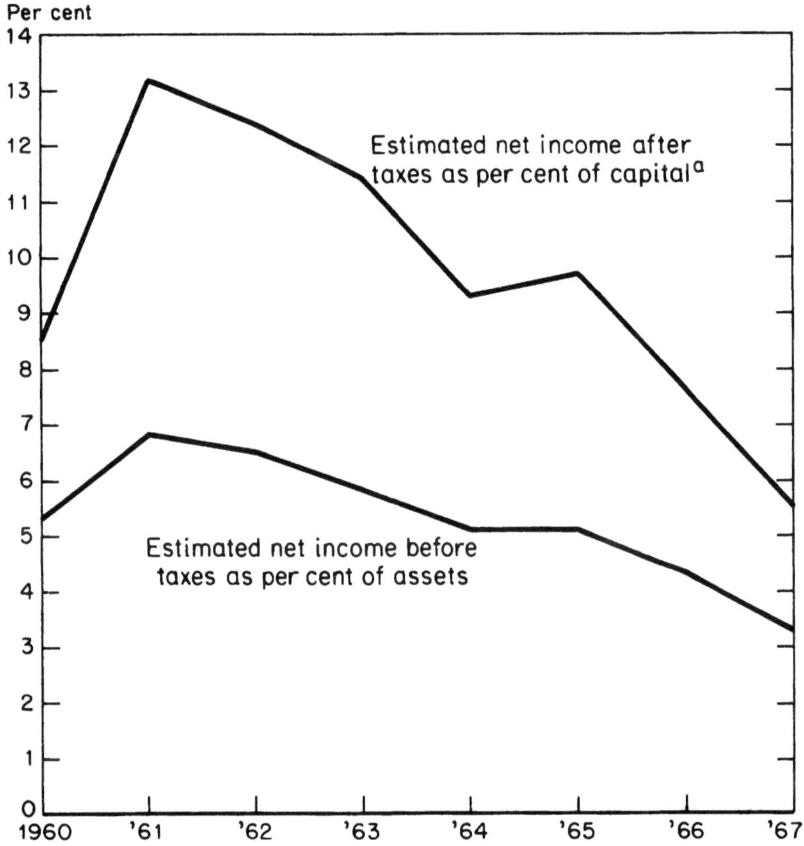

SOURCE: Table 21.
[a] End-of-year capital in 1960.

TABLE 21
Estimated Return on Average Assets and Capital Under New York's Small Loan Law, All Licensees, State Totals, 1960-67

	1960	1961	1962	1963	1964	1965	1966	1967
Estimated net income before taxes as per cent of average assets	5.3	6.8	6.5	5.8	5.1	5.1	4.3	3.3
Estimated net income after taxes as per cent of average capital	8.5[a]	13.2	12.4	11.4	9.3	9.7	7.6	5.5

Source: New York State Consumer Finance Association and National Consumer Finance Association data. Estimates made by the authors.
[a] End-of-year capital.

in 1957.[10] These estimates are, of course, subject to error if the following assumptions are incorrect: first, that the relative proportions of borrowed funds and equity capital for all interstate companies operating as licensed lenders in New York are the same, on average, as those for consumer finance companies in each size category reporting to the National Consumer Finance Association; second, that the interest charges and federal taxes for interstate companies operating in New York bear the same proportion to average outstanding assets as those for consumer finance companies reporting to the NCFA.

Given these qualifications, we note that one year after the 1960 amendment to the small loan law, the return rose from 8 to 13 per cent, declining thereafter to a 1967 low of 5.5 per cent. After 1965, it is apparent that the incentive to invest capital, measured by return on equity, had lost all of the stimulus received from the 1960 amendment.

[10] The Chapman-Jones study (*op. cit.*, p. 14) based its estimates upon still narrower assumptions than ours: (1) That the relative proportions of borrowed funds and equity capital for all licensed lenders in New York taken together are the same as those found in the annual reports of the five largest national organizations for which appropriate data are available; (2) that interest charges of all licensed lenders bear the same relation to net operating income before taxes and before interest as is the case with these larger parent companies; and (3) that federal taxes take the same proportion of net operating income before interest and before taxes as in the larger parent companies.

The Financial Status of Licensed Lenders in New York, 1960-67

It would appear from the foregoing measures of return on assets and equity, before and after taxes, that the regulation of licensed lending in New York is maintained by offsetting higher returns in "good" years (shortly after amendments to the small loan law are made) with "lean" years (when sub-par returns are earned by licensed lenders who wait for further relief from the legislature).

When rate and loan ceilings are fixed in relation to costs at a particular point of time, they gradually become obsolete as market forces alter cost-revenue relationships. New York, by providing protected markets for licensees, offers hope that changes in legislation will let lenders average out the good and lean years. While it is obvious from our data that lean years have again arrived, we question whether the philosophy of limiting competition in this manner provides an effective environment for providing loans to consumer borrowers. As of now, we can only state that any adjustments made by licensed lenders to offset the pressures of rising costs have not succeeded in preventing the deterioration of the profitability of licensed lending and the incentive to attract capital between 1961 and 1967.

IV

Factors Affecting the Profitability of Licensed Lending in New York State, 1960-67

In Chapter 3, the combination of rising operating expenses and declining gross income portrayed a squeeze upon net income before interest and taxes. Further, rising interest costs accentuated the pressure of costs upon net income before taxes. Expenses can be paid only out of income; therefore, when expenses rise in relation to income there is a squeeze on profits unless volume rises sufficiently to allow profits to be maintained or increased. No such rise in the volume of business occurred to offset the worsening expense-income relation after 1961.

In order to analyze these developments, we shall review the movements of the major expense components expressed as percentages of income, rather than in per cent of average loans outstanding.[1] It may then be possible to observe whether licensed lenders adjusted uniformly to the changing conditions, or whether adjustments in their

[1] This procedure has been used for the following reasons. First expressing individual expense items as percentages of gross income is advantageous because it indicates the proportion of income that is required to cover expenses of a particular kind. Second, expressing the expense components as percentages of gross income shows *directly* the relation between income and expenses. When an expense measure is shown in terms of average loans outstanding (A.L.O.), it is necessary to examine two measures to ascertain its effect upon operating profits—gross income as a percentage of A.L.O. and expense components as percentages of A.L.O. Expenses expressed as percentages of gross income are therefore more conducive to perception of the effects of the profit squeeze.

financial structure occurred to cushion the effects upon the return to equity.

To accomplish these ends, we express the three major expense components for our sample of companies in percentage of gross income: operating expenses, excluding bad debts; bad debts; and interest expense. Together, these three items represented 78 per cent of gross income for our sample of companies in 1967. Finally, we review the estimated changes in debt-equity ratios among these companies.

Operating Expense as a Percentage of Gross Income

Historically, operating expense, excluding bad debts, has declined dramatically as a percentage of gross income since 1945.[2] The downward movement was reversed during the 1960-67 period. With the passage of small loan legislation in 1960, there was an initial decline from 43.5 per cent to 38.2 per cent in 1961 followed by an upward movement of the ratio to 45 per cent in 1967 (Chart 16 and Table 22). Among components of operating expense, the rise of salaries in relation to gross income was somewhat larger than the rise in other expenses, although the trend was similar for both categories during the period. The economies in expense that might be expected when lenders lend larger amounts did not materialize. The larger average loan sizes outstanding after 1961 did not provide sufficient added revenue from the ¾ per cent bracket of New York's rate ceiling structure to cover the added expenses incurred. Since operating expenses were relatively stable as a percentage of average loans outstanding during the period, the declining income rather than an upward surge of expenses seems primarily responsible for the profit squeeze.

Charts 17, 18, and 19 and Tables 23, 24, and 25 reveal that the

[2] Using state data for selected years, the following is illustrative:

Year	*Operating Expense-Income Ratio*
1946	56.8
1955	51.7
1959	47.6
1960	44.7
1967	47.3

CHART 16
Operating Expenses as a Percentage of Gross Income, All Sample Companies, 1960-67

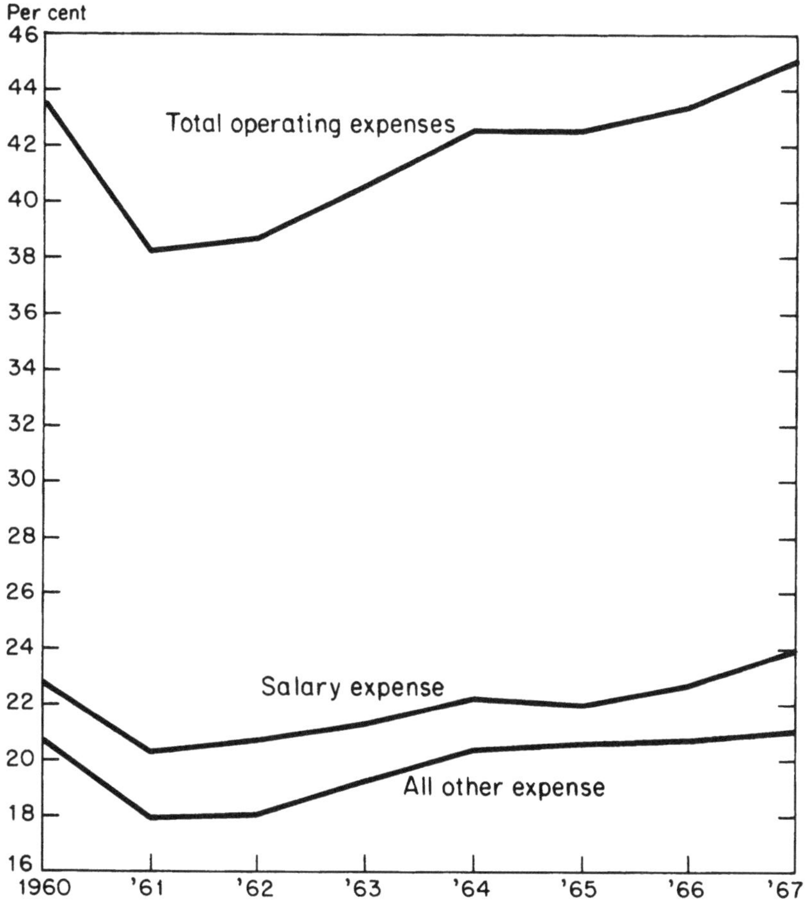

SOURCE: Table 22.

TABLE 22
Operating Expenses as a Percentage of Gross Income, All Sample Companies, 1960-67

	1960	1961	1962	1963	1964	1965	1966	1967
Total operating expenses	43.5	38.2	38.7	40.6	42.6	42.6	43.4	45.0
Salary expense	22.8	20.3	20.7	21.3	22.2	22.0	22.7	24.0
All other	20.7	17.9	18.0	19.3	20.4	20.6	20.7	21.0

Source: New York State Consumer Finance Association.

expense-income trend for all sample companies reflects more closely the experience of the very large company size group rather than that of the other two size groups. Although the large company group showed the most unfavorable experience between 1960 and 1967, it occurred primarily because of the salary expense ratio in 1967, an event attributable to special factors, which can be disregarded here.[3] Until 1967, all three groups did reasonably well in keeping their operating expenses in relation to gross income close to their 1960 levels while the average size of loans outstanding increased during the period (Table 26). But, after 1961, there occurred a consistent narrowing of operating profit margins as operating expenses rose in relation to gross income. The very large company size group maintained lower level operating expense ratios to gross income throughout. In 1967, these ratios had rise above their 1960 levels for all but the medium-sized companies.

It is possible that licensed lenders could have adjusted to the increasing expense-income relationship in several ways. First, they might have raised their credit standards so that only the better credit risks were accepted for loans. Chart 20 and Table 27 reveal that this did not happen. The ratio of bad debts to gross income rose irregularly from 6.6 per cent in 1960 to 7.3 per cent in 1967 for the very large companies while the other two groups had adverse chargeoffs both in 1960 and 1967. The greater variability in bad debt ratios for the large and medium size groups suggests that they were not able to control their

[3] One company in this group sold a number of offices in 1967, raising the proportion of salary expense to gross income.

CHART 17
Operating Expenses as a Percentage of Gross Income, Very Large Companies, 1960-67

SOURCE: Table 23.

CHART 18
Operating Expenses as a Percentage of Gross Income, Large Companies, 1960-67

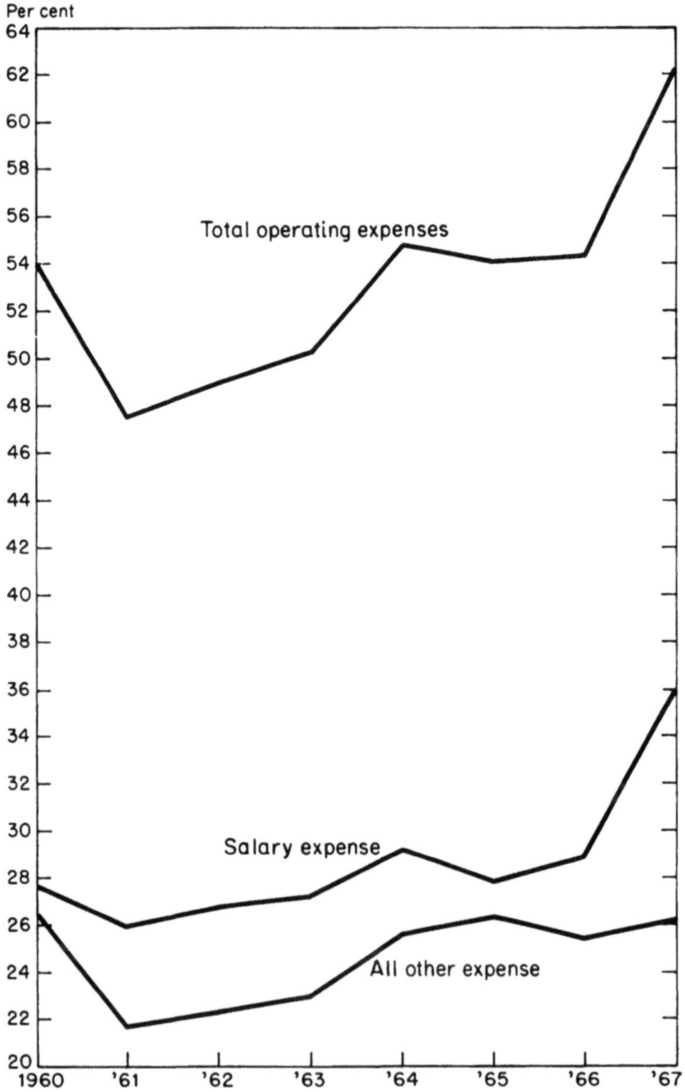

SOURCE: Table 24.

CHART 19
Operating Expenses as a Percentage of Gross Income, Medium-Sized Companies, 1960-67

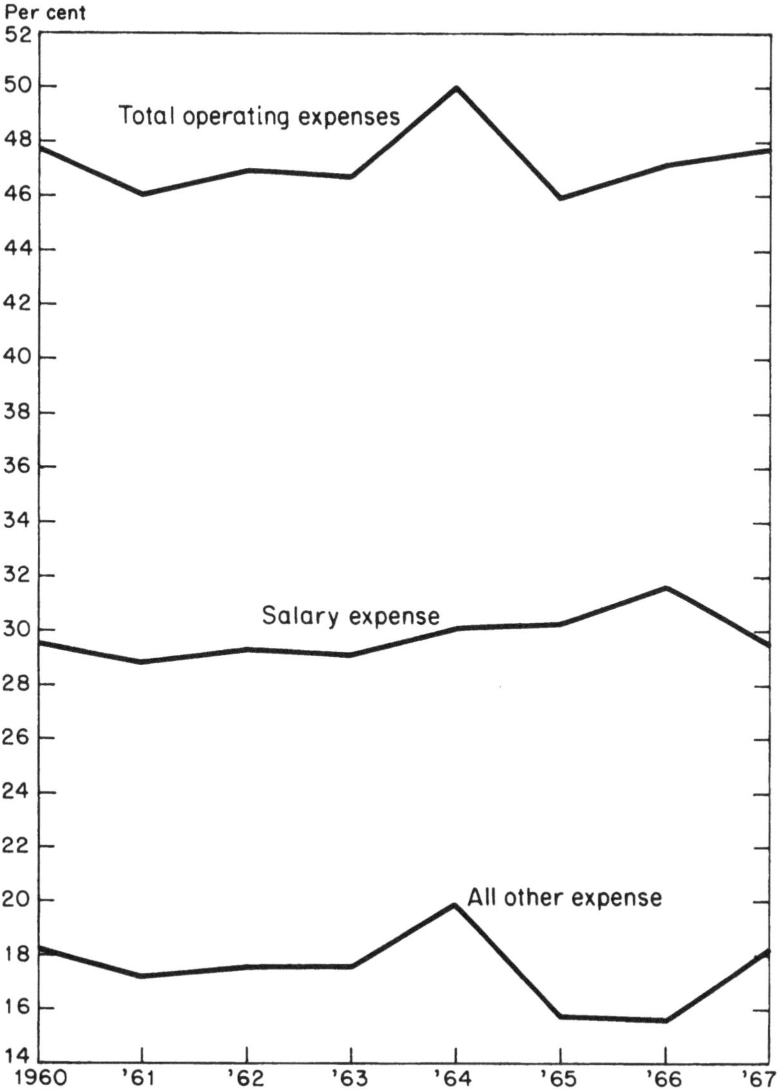

Source: Table 25.

TABLE 23
Operating Expenses as a Percentage of Gross Income, Very Large Companies, 1960-67

	1960	1961	1962	1963	1964	1965	1966	1967
Total operating expenses	42.2	37.0	37.3	39.4	41.1	41.3	42.1	43.4
Salary expense	22.1	19.5	19.8	20.5	21.3	21.2	21.8	22.8
All other	20.1	17.5	17.5	18.9	19.8	20.1	20.3	20.6

Source: New York State Consumer Finance Association.

TABLE 24
Operating Expense as a Percentage of Gross Income, Large Companies, 1960-67

	1960	1961	1962	1963	1964	1965	1966	1967
Total operating expenses	54.0	47.5	49.0	50.2	54.8	54.1	54.3	62.2
Salary expense	27.6	25.9	26.7	27.2	29.2	27.8	28.9	36.0
All other	26.4	21.6	22.3	23.0	25.6	26.3	25.4	26.2

Source: New York State Consumer Finance Association.

TABLE 25
Operating Expenses as a Percentage of Gross Income, Medium-Sized Companies, 1960-67

	1960	1961	1962	1963	1964	1965	1966	1967
Total operating expenses	47.7	46.0	46.9	46.7	50.0	45.9	47.2	47.7
Salary expense	29.5	28.8	29.3	29.1	30.1	30.2	31.6	29.5
All other	18.2	17.2	17.6	17.6	19.9	15.7	15.6	18.2

Source: New York State Consumer Finance Association.

TABLE 26
Average Size of Loans Outstanding for Sample Companies, 1959-67
(dollars)

Year	Total Sample	Very Large	Large	Medium
1959	309.7	312.4	287.0	295.1
1960	346.3	348.5	331.4	327.6
1961	388.9	390.9	377.1	367.3
1962	411.9	414.2	398.6	388.6
1963	430.4	432.3	418.4	400.7
1964	441.9	443.5	430.3	419.3
1965	453.9	455.4	442.5	438.9
1966	473.2	476.0	452.1	450.8
1967	483.6	485.7	455.6	457.1

Source: New York State Consumer Finance Association.

credit risks as successfully as the larger companies during the period (Table 27).

Two conclusions emerge from the foregoing. First, net bad debt charges as a percentage of gross income contributed to, and did not relieve, the squeeze on profit margins during the period. Second, the two smaller size groups experienced higher and more variable bad debt charges than the very large companies between 1960 and 1967.

It is possible that licensed lenders did not cut down on the credit worthiness of borrowers accepted for loans, as they did after 1941, because such a course of action might have been self-defeating. Cutting down on the number of customers served in a state where the rate ceiling structure requires full utilization of offices to operate profitably could have worsened their position if operating costs per dollar of revenue rose more than net bad debt charges declined. With higher profit margins than those indicated for companies in the two smaller size groups, the very large companies could better afford to maintain their market position despite the unfavorable trend of expenses and wait for eventual legislative relief.

CHART 20
Net Bad Debt Charge as a Percentage of Gross Income, 1960-67

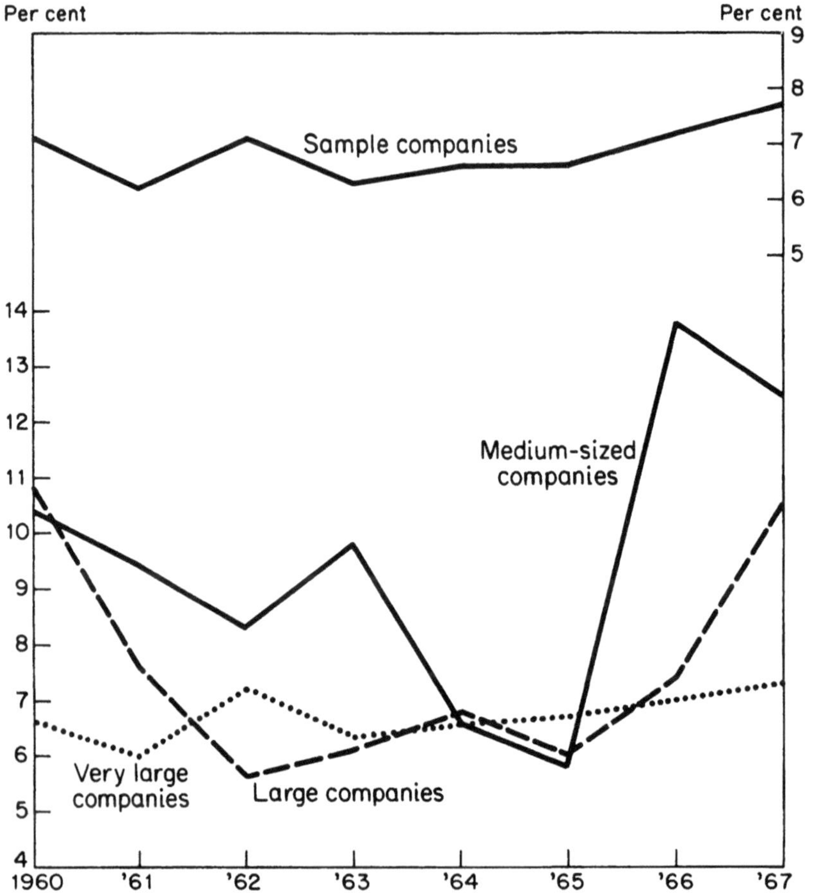

Source: Table 27.

TABLE 27
Net Bad Debt Charge as a Percentage of Gross Income, 1960-67

	1960	1961	1962	1963	1964	1965	1966	1967
All sample companies	7.1	6.2	7.1	6.3	6.6	6.6	7.2	7.7
Very large companies	6.6	6.0	7.2	6.3	6.6	6.7	7.0	7.3
Large companies	10.8	7.6	5.6	6.1	6.8	6.0	7.4	10.5
Medium companies	10.4	9.4	8.3	9.8	6.6	5.8	13.8	12.5

Source: New York State Consumer Finance Association.

Interest Expense as a Percentage of Gross Income

The last opportunity for sample companies in general, and the very large companies in particular, to offset the effects of declining operating profits, before taxes, would be if the factor over which they have little control, interest, had declined in relation to income. But, as already noted, interest expense rose markedly during the period and especially in 1966 and 1967. For sample companies as a whole, estimated interest expense increased from 19.7 to 25.6 per cent of gross income between 1960 and 1967 (Chart 21 and Table 28). For the very large companies, the estimated increase was the most sizeable, accentuating the squeeze on profits. The medium-sized companies, on the other hand, held their 1967 ratio of estimated interest to gross income to 22.5 per cent contrasting with the 25.3 and 28.3 per cent relation to gross income for the large and very large companies respectively.[4] The very large companies had substantially lower borrowing costs in 1960 and must have been greatly affected by the increases in the prime rate in 1966 and 1967 to substantially higher levels than the 5 per cent prime rate that existed between January 1960 and August

[4] The large company group was reduced to three companies for this calculation.

CHART 21
Estimated Interest Expense as a Percentage of Gross Income, 1960-67

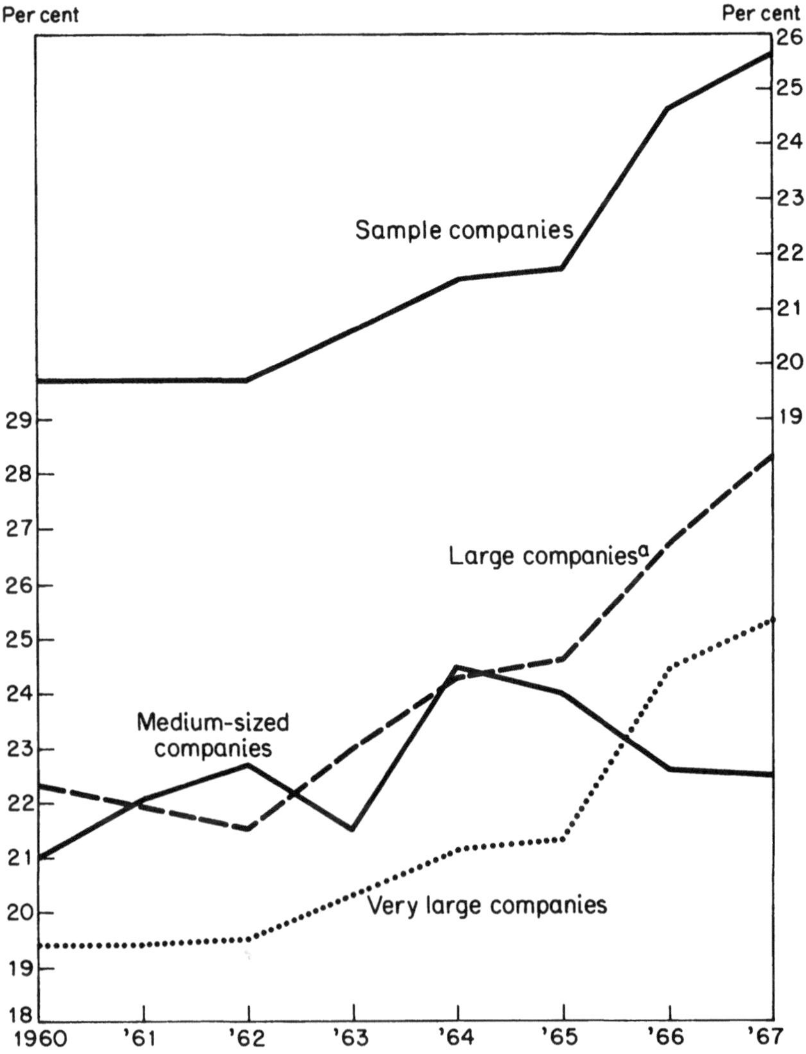

SOURCE: Table 28.
[a] One of four companies was not included in 1967.

TABLE 28
Estimated Interest Expense as a Percentage of Gross Income, 1960-67

	1960	1961	1962	1963	1964	1965	1966	1967
Sample companies	19.7	19.7	19.7	20.6	21.5	21.7	24.6	25.6
Very large companies	19.4	19.4	19.5	20.3	21.1	21.3	24.4	25.3
Large companies	22.3	21.9	21.5	23.0	24.3	24.6	26.7	28.3[a]
Medium-sized companies	21.0	22.1	22.7	21.5	24.5	24.0	22.6	22.5

Source: New York State Consumer Finance Association and National Consumer Finance Association data. Estimates made by the authors.

[a] One of four companies was not included in this calculation.

1965. The large and medium size companies apparently did not gain the benefit of low prime rates in the early part of the period and did not experience as sharp a rise in their borrowing costs.

It is apparent that the very large companies, in particular, did not compensate for reduced operating profit margins by cutting down on bad debt and interest expense. How, then, did they react to the squeeze on profit margins? Did they attempt to grow faster than the other size groups? We have already noted that this was not the case. Did they trade more heavily on their equity to maintain the return to their shareholders? For interstate companies, this, of course, would be a decision taken with respect to their national operations and would not be made solely on the basis of their New York experience. But, once made, such a decision could affect their behavior in New York and might differentiate their policies from those of the intrastate companies.

Changes in the Estimated Financial Structure of Licensed Lenders in New York, 1960-67

Estimates of changes in the financial structure of New York's licensed lenders supports the thesis that by borrowing a higher proportion of total funds, they were able to maintain a higher rate of return on capital than if they had not done so. Table 29 reveals that New

York's sample companies, under the pressure of rising costs, maintained their net operating income ratio to total assets better than they maintained the corresponding ratio to average loans outstanding (see Table 16). This could only have been accomplished by lowering the proportion of nonearning assets. Further, although there was a sharp decline in the estimated net return on borrowed funds, the increase in the estimated ratio of borrowed funds to capital prevented the return on capital from declining more sharply. Using 1967 to illustrate, the return on average total assets was 9.0 per cent. By subtracting the estimated cost of borrowed funds from 9.0 per cent we assume that the remainder, 2.7 per cent, represents the net return that borrowed funds contributes to equity. The actual size of the contribution to equity depends upon the proportion of borrowed funds to equity. If the 1960 estimated ratio of borrowed funds to equity had existed in 1967, and if the 1967 proportion of taxes is applied to the before-tax return on equity, the 1967 return on equity would have been 7.2 instead of 7.8 per cent[5] Thus, the rise from a 3.30 to a 3.75 ratio of borrowed funds to equity offset a portion of the decline in the return on assets.

Greater leverage in the financial structure of any firm represents increasing risk to creditors and accentuates the variability of returns to stockholders. Yet increased risk was not accompanied by increased reward since the estimated after-tax return on capital in 1967 was below the 1960 level despite the increased ratio of borrowed funds to net worth.

Table 29 reveals that the medium-sized companies increased their leverage ratio to the greatest extent, both in absolute and proportionate terms. The very large companies increased their leverage ratio somewhat less, while the large companies' increase was the least. Between 1965 and 1967, the large companies actually decreased their dependence upon borrowed funds. If they had not done so, their interest expense would have been a higher proportion of gross income.

[5] The method of calculation is to multiply the estimated net return on borrowed funds by the ratio of borrowed funds to equity, add to the product the average return on total assets, and multiply this ratio by one minus the 1967 proportion of taxes to net income before taxes. See Paul F. Smith, *Consumer Credit Costs, 1949-1959,* National Bureau of Economic Research, New York, 1964, Table 6, p. 20, for a similar calculation.

TABLE 29
Estimated Return on Assets and Capital Invested Under New York's Small Loan Law, Sample Companies, 1960-67
(per cent)

	1960	1961	1962	1963	1964	1965	1966	1967
Net operating income before interest and taxes divided by average total assets	9.9	11.7	11.0	10.3	9.8	9.7	9.5	9.0
Less: Estimated interest divided by estimated average borrowed funds	4.7[a]	5.4	5.3	5.3	5.3	5.4	6.0	6.3
Equals: Estimated net return on borrowed funds	n.a.	6.3	5.7	5.0	4.5	4.5	3.5	2.7
Estimated ratio of borrowed to capital funds	3.30	3.11	3.25	3.40	3.63	3.51	3.57	3.75
Very large companies	3.26	3.03	3.18	3.33	3.52	3.41	3.48	3.72
Large companies	4.02	3.84	3.86	4.16	4.46	4.55	4.44	4.21
Medium-sized companies	2.99	3.12	3.06	2.99	n.a.	3.72	3.37	3.54
Estimated net income after taxes as per cent of capital funds	9.1[a]	14.8	12.8	11.4	10.2	11.1	8.2	7.8

Source: New York State Consumer Finance Association and National Consumer Finance Association data. Estimates made by the authors.

[a] Year-end estimates of balance sheet items.

n.a. = not available.

We conclude by noting that changes in the financial structure, along with more efficient use of cash and other nonearning assets, helped maintain returns to capital in New York to the levels shown. But these adjustments have not been sufficient to overcome the forces decreasing the estimated return to capital, which has apparently fallen below the 1960 level.

V

Practices Accompanying Regulation of Licensed Lending in New York

As noted earlier, New York ranks either lowest or close to lowest with respect to the height of the permissible rate ceiling among 47 states[1] Also, 31 out of the 47 states with effective small loan laws had higher loan limits than New York's $800 loan limit in January 1968. Since the combination of restrictive rate and loan size limits characterizes New York's law, this chapter examines some of the practices that have grown up under these constraints.

Fragmentary data were collected to identify practices that evade the intent of restrictive legislation in New York. Time and budget limitations precluded a more thorough investigation. But the evidence does corroborate what an economic analysis of restrictive legal limits placed on any market would suggest: first, that borrowers will seek alternative arrangements to accomplish their desired objectives; second, that institutional arrangements will be offered within the law where possible, to give the borrower what he wants at a price that will cover costs and return a profit; and finally, higher-cost sources of credit will arise to satisfy needs that cannot be met by licensed loans under restrictive statutes.

We deal with each of these possibilities in turn. First of all, we shall see how borrowers evade the intent of the $800 loan limit by

[1] Sec Table 5.

"doubling up" on their loans – making loans from more than one consumer finance company. Second, we shall see how borrowers can go to adjacent states with more permissive laws while lenders in those states may advertise the availability of those loans in the state with a restrictive law. Third, we shall explore whether borrowers in poorer areas are made more dependent upon the blandishments of low-quality credit retailers for household goods or are driven to loan sharks for emergency loans because they lack comparable opportunities for licensed loans.

Doubled-Up Loans, 1957 and 1968

In 1957, the Banking Department requested two large national consumer finance companies to investigate the per cent of all open accounts in New York that were doubled with those of other lenders. They reported that "approximately 18 per cent of all open accounts at small loan licensees were doubled with other lenders. Over 60 per cent occurred where the original loan was made at the ceiling maximum of $500." [2]

Our current investigation of doubled loans from consumer finance companies suggest that the percentage of total accounts that were doubled in September-October 1968 was about 22.3 per cent, considerably higher than in September 1957. Our first evidence was collected by taking small samples of accounts reported to the lenders' exchanges for the consumer finance industry both in Buffalo and in New York City.[3] As shown in Table 30, the per cent of doubled loans did not vary appreciably between New York City and the upstate area.

Further investigation based upon the downstate accounts in New York held by one national lender revealed that 8,798 of 37,407 outstanding accounts, or 23.5 per cent, were double-ups during August 1968. The closeness of this result with that from the sample collected at the lenders' exchanges reinforces the conclusion that the proportion of borrowers meeting their needs by multiple borrowing had risen to approximately 22 or 23 per cent, or well beyond the 18 per cent level

[2] *An Analysis of the Licensed Lender Industry, op. cit.*, 1957, p. 20.

[3] The sampling procedure followed in New York City was to draw one card (account) from each of 1,040 boxes of cards. (Cards were arranged alphabetically in the 1,040 boxes). In Buffalo, a similar procedure was followed: 15 cards were drawn from each of 66 boxes.

TABLE 30
Number and Percentage of Doubled Accounts at Lenders' Exchanges, Fall 1967

Location	Number of Accounts in Sample	Number of Doubled Accounts in Sample	Per Cent of Total Accounts Doubled
New York City	1,040	219	21.1
Buffalo	990	233	23.5
Total	2,030	452	22.3

Source: Samples drawn at Lenders' Exchanges and Tabulated by Thomas A. Durkin.

reached in 1959, shortly before the loan limit was increased from $500 to $800 in New York.

Choosing four New York City offices on 42nd Street that cater to both East Side and West Side commuters, we further investigated the distribution of doubled accounts by intervals based upon the size of the borrower's combined loans from consumer finance companies,[4] and median monthly income. Table 31 reveals that 54 per cent of the doubled accounts totaled $1,600 or more, suggesting that both loans were made at a similar point in time for the maximum amount of $800.[5] For these borrowers, the effective limit of the New York small loan law was $1,600, not $800. Further, borrowers paid an effective rate of 19 per cent per annum for the loan of $1,600, which is the same as that paid for a loan of $800.[6] Finally, they incurred the added inconvenience and paid the costs of two separate credit investigations, separate servicing, and collection expenses involved in the extension of two loans. The median monthly income of these borrowers was $650.

Borrowers receiving more than $800 and less than $1,600 at the time when the doubling was reported comprised 42 per cent of the

[4] By custom, licensed lenders in New York will not extend loans to borrowers who the lenders' exchanges report as having more than one loan outstanding from consumer finance companies.

[5] Under precomputation, the interest charged on the loan is added to the principal amount borrowed so the outstanding amount is larger than the amount borrowed. Thus, two $800 loans when made on the same day will total more than $1,600 outstanding on that day.

[6] See Table 5.

TABLE 31
Distribution of Doubled Loan Accounts, Four 42nd Street, New York City, Offices, September-October 1968

Combined Loans Outstanding	Number of Doubled Accounts	Per Cent of Doubled Accounts	Median Monthly Income (dollars)
$1,600 and over	409	54.4	650
$1,200-$1,599	228	30.3	550
$800-$1,199	84	11.2	532
Under $800	31	4.1	480
Total doubled accounts	752	100.0	n.a.
Total accounts	3,382	n.a.	n.a.
Percentage of accounts doubled	22.2	n.a.	n.a.

Source: Two national consumer finance companies' offices.
n.a. = not applicable.

remaining 46 per cent of the double-ups. Some of these borrowers may have borrowed $800 both times but the timing of the second borrowing may have occurred after the first $800 had been reduced by repayment. Finally, the remaining 4 per cent of the double-ups occurred among borrowers who obtained two loans whose combined amount totaled less than the maximum allowed for one loan. These borrowers may have not been able to qualify for a single loan of $800 from one lender but may have been able to qualify for two smaller loans, each of which carries a higher rate under the graduated rate ceiling.[7] Others may have borrowed smaller separate amounts at different times merely for convenience.

It is also noteworthy that the median monthly income of doubled borrowers increases with the size of the combined borrowing. This suggests that licensed lenders regulate the combined borrowing total so that it matches the ability of the borrower to repay such loans. Thus, it would appear that the real loan limit under the New York law is not $800 but $1,600 for those borrowers who can qualify at an effective rate of 19 per cent per annum. But these borrowers are subject to the

[7] Two $400 loans, for example, carry an effective annual rate of 25.08 per cent. See Table 5.

additional inconvenience of borrowing from two lenders, making two sets of payments, and paying a rate of charge consistent with the waste implicit in doubled-up lending mandated by law. To some extent the process of doubling up loans allows borrowers who cannot qualify for credit in larger amounts from lower-cost cash lenders to obtain larger loans. But the process involves wasteful duplication of time and energies, which are shouldered by the borrower in the form of a higher rate of charge and the cost of his own time.

Borrowing in Adjacent States

The joint efforts of borrowers and lenders make borrowing across state lines a feasible alternative for the extension of loans that cannot be provided under New York's restrictive small loan statute. There are two ways that lenders can make the availability of their services known across state lines. First they can advertise the terms of lending and how arrangements can be made with a minimum of travel (see Exhibit 1). Second, in a commuting area a prospective borrower can be advised, for example, in New York City that his account can be handled in one of that company's loan offices in the adjacent state, located close to the commuter's home. In September 1967, New Jersey's loan limit was increased from $500 to $1,000. Before that time, it was advantageous for commuters who wanted to borrow larger amounts than $500 to borrow $800 in New York City if they could qualify for the loan at the 19 per cent per annum rate of charge. There was some slight advantage to borrowing in New Jersey for the marginal borrower who might be turned down in New York because New Jersey's rate was slightly higher than New York's on loans up to $500. After the 1967 change in the New Jersey law, the borrower of larger amounts would find it advantageous to borrow from a loan office close to his home in New Jersey rather than near his place of work in New York City. When the law was changed, many outstanding accounts from loan offices in New York were transferred to the same company's offices in New Jersey. While it cannot be ascertained definitely, it is probable that the absolute decline in loans outstanding in New York in 1967 was in part due to the change in borrowing patterns among residents of the two states. Table 32 reveals that loans outstanding in

EXHIBIT I

The Times Herald RECORD

Weather: Cloudy — Middletown, N.Y. 10940 — Wednesday morning, June 19, 1968 — 10 Cents

LOANS to $3500

Monthly Payment Schedule

CASH TO YOU	48 MOS.	36 MOS.	24 MOS.
$1000.00	-----	36.38	49.75
2000.00	-----	72.22	98.77
3000.00	87.84	108.06	147.79
3500.00	102.41	125.98	172.30

Above payments include principal and interest

Need a larger loan to consolidate your bills, buy a new car, make home repairs, or for any worthy purpose? Call or write Capital Consumer Discount Co. in Matamoras. Your application can be made by letter and the loan completed with just one trip to the office.

CAPITAL CONSUMER DISCOUNT

203 Pennsylvania Ave., Matamoras, Pennsylvania Phone Area Code 717-491-4168

TABLE 32
Change in Loans Outstanding in New York, by Selected Areas, 1967 and 1968
(amounts in thousands of dollars)

	End-of-Year Loans Outstanding		Per Cent Change
	1966	1967	
State of New York	410,401	404,897	- 1.3
Outside New York City	224,967	227,531	+ 1.1
New York City	185,434	177,366	- 3.4
New York City boroughs connected to New Jersey			
Richmond	9,751	7,597	- 22.1
Manhattan	61,215	58,168	- 5.0
Other New York City boroughs			
Bronx	22,883	22,366	- 2.3
Brooklyn	51,512	50,030	- 2.9
Queens	40,073	39,205	- 2.2

Source: New York State Banking Department.

New York City showed a decline while loans outside of New York City actually increased, suggesting that the bulk of cash loan transfers from New York to New Jersey contributed to New York's first decline in loans outstanding since 1942. Further, within New York City, the two boroughs connected by bridges or tunnels to New Jersey showed larger percentage decreases in loans outstanding than the city-wide average.

The largest differential in loan limits between New York and its adjacent states occurs with Pennsylvania whose Consumer Discount Company Act allows loans to be made in amounts up to $3,500 with repayments scheduled over a maximum term of 4 years and 15 days. Exhibit 1 provides an example of how lenders can communicate to borrowers the advantages of crossing state lines to provide a credit service not allowed at comparable rates in the adjacent state. First, the ad appears in a Middletown, New York, newspaper, a town approximately 20 miles from the Pennsylvania border. The town of Matamoras, Pennsylvania, where the loan office is located, is virtually on the border where the New York, New Jersey, and Pennsylvania boundaries meet. Second, only amounts in excess of those allowed under the New York and New Jersey statutes are advertised, and the costs of these loans are higher than those of the institutions in New York that are allowed to make consumer loans in amounts between $800 and $5,000. Third, the advertisement indicates that only one trip to the office is necessary to obtain the loan since applications can be made by mail in advance.

While such evidence suggests that borrowing across state lines exists, we selected a few communities along the New York and Pennsylvania border where two national companies had offices on both sides of the border to see whether their loan accounts in Pennsylvania contained more New York state borrowers than their New York office contained Pennsylvania borrowers. Table 33 indicates mixed results. One loan office in Sayre, Pennsylvania, had the highest percentage (38 per cent) of total accounts from New York. Nearby New York offices in Elmira, New York, had eight or nine per cent of their total accounts from Pennsylvania residents. In one Warren, Pennsylvania, office, 18 per cent of total accounts were from New York borrowers, while in the other, the corresponding per cent was much lower. The closest matching New York office, Jamestown, had a much lower per cent (1 per cent) of Pennsylvania accounts than the other New York offices sampled. Finally, the pairing of offices in Bradford, Pennsylvania, with an office in Olean, New York, did not produce significant differences, possibly because the geographical distances between the two communities was greater and the road connections are not as direct as in the other pairings.

Although the evidence is skimpy, we conclude that borrowing across state lines can be appreciable in response to differences between state laws when the traveling distance is relatively small and when lenders communicate the availability of loan services to borrowers in adjacent states. In all of the border Pennsylvania communities investigated there was an appreciable percentage of New York accounts that were heavily concentrated in loan sizes above the legal limit for licensed lenders operating in New York.

TABLE 33
Percentage of Out-of-State Accounts in Loan Offices Located in Selected Border Communities, New York and Pennsylvania, December 1968
(per cent)

	Pennsylvania Accounts in New York Offices	New York Accounts in Pennsylvania Offices		
		Total	Above $800	Below $800
Sayre, Pennsylvania	n.a.	38	24	14
Elmira, New York	8	n.a.	n.a.	n.a.
Elmira, New York	9	n.a.	n.a.	n.a.
Warren, Pennsylvania	n.a.	6	6	0
Warren, Pennsylvania	n.a.	18	18	0
Jamestown, New York	1	n.a.	n.a.	n.a.
Bradford, Pennsylvania	n.a.	8	5	3
Bradford, Pennsylvania	n.a.	8	8	0
Olean, New York	8	n.a.	n.a.	n.a.

Source: Two national companies with offices in both states.
n.a. = not applicable.

Availability of Loans to Borrowers in Poorer Areas

One of the unfortunate aspects of a small loan statute that has restrictive rate ceilings is that it cuts down the availability of loans in poorer areas. In these areas, borrowers who cannot qualify for cash loans typically have the choice of purchasing low-quality goods at inflated prices or of patronizing the neighborhood loan sharks. David Caplovitz, in his study of the credit purchases of the inhabitants of settlement houses in East Harlem and on the lower East Side of New York, has documented the prevalence of such practices in the merchandising of goods, while the existence and prevalence of loan sharks is acknowledged only by word of mouth.[8] Unfortunately, today's re-

[8] *The Poor Pay More*, New York, 1963, Chapter 10.

stricted credit availability in these areas takes on a racial composition only because nonwhites have moved into these marginal city areas inhabited by lower-income groups after the earlier white immigrants from abroad moved out.

We requested information from two national companies with offices in New York to see whether the percentage of loans approved varied according to the socioeconomic character of the area served. Because data on average income of borrowers per office were not readily available, we classified offices according to the relative frequency of nonwhite customers among their loan accounts outstanding. Table 34 reveals that when offices are grouped according to whether customers were predominantly white, majority white, majority nonwhite, or predominantly nonwhite, the percentage of applications approved declined as the predominance of nonwhite accounts held rose. That this may be an income, rather than a racial phenomenon is indicated by the location of the offices included. The predominantly white and majority white suburban offices are located, for the most part, in moderate or higher-income areas. The predominantly nonwhite and majority nonwhite offices are located in the poorer areas of New York City. The relevant point to be made by the lower percentage of applications approved in the poorer areas is that the costs incurred in rejecting loan applications must be recovered from the revenues paid by those whose applications are accepted. As a result, the costs of extending loans in the poorer areas run higher in relation to the permissible rate ceiling, and the number of offices and availability of loans is cut down correspondingly. In the areas where the traditional kind of "small loan" is needed most, the low rate ceiling makes it more difficult to make loans that will result in the customary return on capital available in other locations.

We have seen that the $800 loan limit in New York is evaded by borrowers in several ways. It is questionable whether a loan limit of any kind serves a useful purpose. One has to go back to the 1946 report of the New York State Banking Department to find a statement as to why such a limit exists. It follows:

> Four different types of institutions now have the authority to make loans in limited amounts at rates of more than 6 percent a year. They are the licensed lenders, industrial banks, credit unions and the personal loan departments of commercial banks. Their fields of higher rate loans are now fairly well marked off. These other instrumentalities are authorized to make the larger loans at rates of interest substantially lower than li-

TABLE 34
Per Cent of Applications Approved in Offices Located in Selected Areas, Two National Companies, August 1968

Office Category and Location	Per Cent of Applications Approved
Seven suburban offices	
Group 1—Predominantly White Customers Hicksville, Levittown (2 offices), and Yorktown Heights	46
Group 2—Majority of White Customers Lindenhurst, Hempstead, and Pleasantville	37
Eight New York City offices	
Group 3—Majority of Non-white Customers Manhattan (Delancey St.), and Brownsville (Linden Blvd.)	35
Group 4—Predominantly Non-White Customers Manhattan (125th St.) (3rd Ave.), Bronx (149th St.) (149th St.), and Brooklyn (Broadway) (Broadway)	33

Source: Two national consumer finance companies.

censed lenders charge. There is no need of creating duplication and overlapping of loan facilities by permitting licensed lenders to cater to income groups able to obtain credit elsewhere at rates that are but one-half to one-quarter of those charged by licensed lenders.[9]

The last sentence of this statement reveals that a fundamental characteristic of any market has been ignored. Licensed lenders who are allowed to charge rates at ceilings substantially higher than those charged by other institutional lenders will attract borrowers who cannot qualify for credit from these other lenders. Today, with a better educated citizenry and compulsory disclosure of rate of charge, there is less likelihood that licensed lenders will attract bank and credit union customers. Instead, once alternative forms of evasion have been exhausted, borrowers who cannot get loans from the lower-cost sources must go without loans, or seek higher-cost retail credit sources and loan sharks. That there is a demand for licensed loans in excess of $800 is evidenced by our data on double-ups. It is also clear that

[9] *Special Report of the Superintendent of Banks on Licensed Lenders, op. cit.,* 1946, p. 20.

licensed lenders ration the doubled borrowing according to the ability of the borrower to carry the indebtedness. Under these circumstances, it would seem that licensed lenders, rather than the state, determine who can qualify for larger loans.

But, again, the height of the rate ceilings is crucial. The higher the rate ceiling structure, the more leeway exists for licensed lenders to make loans to borrowers who, as a group, appear to be substandard credit risks under lower rate ceilings. Within these groups are many credit-worthy borrowers who are denied credit because lenders cannot determine in advance which borrowers will be unable to repay. The impact of New York's relatively low rate ceiling structure falls upon credit-worthy marginal borrowers who congregate in areas where people of like financial circumstances reside. Fewer loan offices will locate in these disadvantaged areas while those that do must, of necessity, skim the cream among credit applicants according to criteria of income, job stability, and other standards used to evaluate loan applications.

Table 35 indicates the dimensions of the problem for two low-income, racially-segregated areas of New York City: Harlem and Bedford-Stuyvesant. Both of these communities represent a mix of industrial, commercial, and residential land-uses exposed to the encroachment of blight and decay. In 1960, more than 60 per cent of all families in Manhattan's Harlem area had incomes of less than $5,000 and 45 per cent had incomes of less than $4,000.[10] Bedford-Stuyvesant is an area within the Borough of Brooklyn that is one of twenty-six major poverty districts in New York City as defined by the city's Human Resources Administration.

Table 35 reveals that there were only three licensed loan offices in the Harlem area in 1967 and three offices in Bedford-Stuyvesant. Because of the greater population in Harlem than in Bedford-Stuyvesant, the population per office ratio in Harlem is considerably higher than in Bedford-Stuyvesant.[11] Yet the ratio for each community is well above the ratio for the Boroughs within which they are located (Manhattan and Brooklyn), and above the corresponding ratios for New

[10] *Report of the Mayor's Task Force for the Economic Redevelopment of Harlem,* submitted January 16, 1968, City of New York, pp. II-14ff.

[11] One of the three offices in Bedford-Stuyvesant has applied to the Banking Department for permission to move outside the area. There is a fourth licensed loan office just adjacent to the boundary, however.

TABLE 35
Comparison of Population Per Licensed Loan Office Ratios in Two Disadvantaged Communities With Ratios in New York City and New York State

Area	Number of Licensed Loan Offices, 1967	Population Estimate[a]	Population Per Office
Harlem[b]	3	495,728	165,243
Bedford-Stuyvesant[c]	3	256,901	85,634
Boroughs of:			
Manhattan	54	1,625,000	30,093
Brooklyn	55	2,600,000	47,273
Bronx	23	1,400,000	60,870
Queens	56	1,875,000	33,482
Richmond	11	250,000	22,727
Total, New York City	199	7,750,000	38,945
Total, New York State	541	17,651,700	32,628

Source: New York State Banking Department; Report of Mayor's Task Force; and Bureau of the Census, U. S. Department of Commerce.

[a] Population estimates are for the year 1965, except for Harlem, which is 1967.
[b] Harlem extends from 110th Street in Manhattan just north of Central Park to 168th Street. Its east-west boundaries are formed by the East, Harlem and Hudson rivers.
[c] Bedford-Stuyvesant is the area of Brooklyn defined by the Human Resources Administration of New York City for the purpose of establishing a community corporation.

York City, and New York State as well.

Thus, we conclude that the major effect of New York's low small loan rate ceiling is to deny loans, rather than to lower the cost of loans, to segments of the population that have traditionally been liberated from the grasp of illegal lenders by the passage of small loan statutes modelled upon the Uniform Small Loan Law. We further believe that New York State's restrictive small loan law has encouraged potential borrowers to patronize low-quality, high mark-up retail credit establishments, which proliferate in areas like Harlem and Bedford-Stuyvesant. Finally, we further believe, but cannot prove, that illegal lending is rampant in areas where borrowers cannot qualify for licensed loans under the present legal rate ceilings, especially for amounts of $300 or less.

Index

Bei Fragen zur Produktsicherheit wenden Sie sich bitte an:
If you have any questions regarding product safety,
please contact:

Walter de Gruyter GmbH
Genthiner Straße 13
10785 Berlin
productsafety@degruyterbrill.com